"Katara Patton's *Navigating the Blues* 90-day devotional is wonderfully transparent and transformational! The concepts and ideas were so useful to me as I faced my own struggles with doubt, fear, and insecurity. I found great comfort in the shared nuggets of practical wisdom, anecdotes, and use of sacred Scripture. As a mental health consumer and advocate, I can attest that Katara Patton's book will bless those who find themselves in need of practical words of guidance and encouragement."

—Rev. Ericka Bailey, speaker, author, and mental health advocate

"*Navigating the Blues* is a welcome resource for Christians who experience depression, anxiety, or other mental health challenges during difficult times. Patton . . . offers encouragement to face the blues with self-compassion, honesty, and faith. The devotional offers practical and relatable strategies that support healing. Patton shares wisdom from her own lived experiences with depression and employs prayer, affirmation, and action to steer readers through common but isolating occurrences of depression."

—Kesha S. Burch, PhD, LCPC, core faculty and staff therapist,
The Family Institute at Northwestern University

"These daily devotions offer acknowledgment, acceptance, affirmation, and assistance. Blending applied wisdom with biblical truth, the author compassionately and capably leads her audience to the One who can safely steer us from deepest blue into the Light."

—Sandra Byrd, author of *The One Year Experiencing
God's Love Devotional*

"Often believers struggle with accepting their negative emotions because they believe that it contradicts their faith. However, *Navigating the Blues* provides space for God's children to be vulnerable without shame or fear as they find comfort for their pain knowing that God hears the cries of His children and will rescue us amid our storms. This book will invite you not only to face those things you have intentionally avoided because of public judgment or self-guilt but also to trust the journey as you begin to heal and experience God's gift of abundant life."

—Jasclyn N. Coney, MA clinical psychology, MDiv

"These devotions provide a safe space to reflect and be vulnerable in overcoming our fears."

—Leticia Ransom, SHRM-CP, PHR, MBA

"*Navigating the Blues* is not only timely; it speaks straight to an issue that so many Christians mask with, 'Too blessed to be stressed (or depressed).' As someone who wrestles with depression and anxiety, I appreciate the author's vulnerability with the 'My Confession' sections. The way the book is structured is easy to navigate and absorb; there are times you barely have enough energy to get out of bed, let alone read God's Word, and when you do, where do you start? Even here, the author directed me to specific Scripture that ministered to that thorn in my side. Lastly, 'Progress, Not Perfection' is a wonderful closing of the daily devotion, providing simple and encouraging steps to be gentle with myself. Katara Washington Patton's *Navigating the Blues* will minister to the heart and heartache of the blues."

—Dr. Stacey Holman, mental health advocate and filmmaker

"Katara Washington Patton has crafted a collection of meditations that touch the existential crisis we face as people of faith. How do we navigate the blues internally and the blues we face externally in our nation? Ms. Patton answers the question with spiritual depth, biblical wisdom, and theological insight. We all as human beings made in God's image will face the blues; the question for people of faith will always be, Can we find the gospel chords among life's blues notes? This book gives us a road map to handling the blue notes and reclaiming our gospel shout!"

—Rev. Dr. Otis Moss III, senior pastor, Trinity United Church of Christ, and professor of homiletics, MacAfee School of Theology

"How I wish I'd had *Navigating the Blues* when I was in the grip of depression. Katara Patton has been there. And she has grappled with the well-meaning but mistaken counsel of fellow believers who were certain that if her faith were strong enough, she would prevail. Full of faith, compassion, understanding, and deep wisdom, these devotions offer comfort, insight, and practical, simple tools to help us move toward wholeness, step-by-step."

—Michelle Rapkin, author and editor

"This much-needed devotional is simply amazing. Depression is a serious issue that the church must pay more attention to. Helps like this offer those who may be suffering a way to confront their issues and begin their healing. I strongly recommend it."

—Rev. Dr. Virgil M. Woods, author and pastor

NAVIGATING THE BLUES

Where to Turn
When Worry, Anxiety,
or Depression
Steals Your Hope

KATARA WASHINGTON PATTON

Our Daily Bread
Publishing™

Navigating the Blues: Where to Turn When Worry, Anxiety, or Depression Steals Your Hope
© 2022 by Katara Washington Patton

The author and publisher are not engaged in rendering medical or psychological services, and this book is not intended as a guide to diagnose or treat medical or psychological problems. If medical, psychological, or other expert assistance is required, the reader should seek the services of a health-care provider or certified counselor.

Interior design by Jody Langley

ISBN: 978-1-64070-207-3

Library of Congress Cataloging-in-Publication Data Available

Printed in the United States of America
23 24 25 26 27 28 29 30 / 9 8 7 6 5 4 3 2

To all my sisters who have wrestled with, or who are currently wrestling with, depression, anxiety, and other mental health challenges. I see you. I pray for you. I appreciate all of my friends who have shared with me your struggles and walked with me on my journey.

CONTENTS

CONTENTS

CONTENTS

INTRODUCTION

Let me begin by stating: I'm a Christian who has suffered with depression for many years. Some of those years I've silently slept more than I care to admit, eaten much more than I should have (especially chocolate), and walked around feeling just numb. Other times, I've taken the advice of a few trusted friends, sought help through psychotherapy, prayed mightily, taken medication, and put into action some of the steps I mention in this book.

Since dealing with my own bouts of depression, I've been troubled by our faith community's response to mental illness for the most part; some, but not all, Christians walk around spouting verses like they are some panacea for anxiety, depression, and other mental illnesses. Until lately (like the past few years), many churches and people of faith haven't even acknowledged that people are suffering from mental illness; they've swept the issue under the rug or, dare I say, under the holy cloth and the holy cloak of being fine (or blessed and highly favored). In addition to rarely seeing our churches collectively assist those suffering with depression, the blues, anxiety, or other mental disorders, I have been told by dear loved ones that all I needed was my Bible and Jesus. Yet, as a person of faith who believes in the power of prayer—and who prayed and prayed for relief—I still suffered. So, what did that say about my faith? How does a Christian keep going when their prayers for relief seem to go unanswered? I didn't question my faith during this time nor did I question God's power to heal me; however, I did keep quiet about how I was feeling sometimes to avoid the Christian quips and "simple" (or should I say insensitive) solutions to a complex illness.

INTRODUCTION

After slowly finding relief from a particular bout, I decided to speak about my experience with the dark cloud known as depression. It was a bold move because many people didn't know I had suffered. I am usually pretty cheerful and upbeat; I wear the mask well—but no one is with me 24/7 except my God, and therefore only God knew what and how I suffered. When I spoke about depression, I received so many confidential messages from friends and acquaintances and even strangers. I had put words to what others were feeling.

One of the most helpful things in this world is to be seen, to be known—not judged but simply known. What I said resonated with many. What I said described some of the feelings others had. And here I was, still standing in my faith, still praying, still seeking and trusting God, yet admitting to being down many days.

That is why I share my story through these reflections. I'm not offering a cure—Lord knows I wish I could. And I'm very clear: I'm not a therapist. But I am a woman who has dealt with depression and reflected on it more days than I'd like to recall. In this devotional, I am offering messages from God's Word that have helped me make it through cloudy days. I'm not erasing faith because I sought help; I'm hopefully displaying how I put faith into action to take steps toward healing—even on days I felt like I was static and not moving or, worse, regressing into my dark place. And that's why after each devotional reflection I've included

- statements for you to repeat (to encourage yourself);
- actions for you to do (progress, not perfection): small steps to push you toward one more step, wholeness, and healing; and
- a prayer to assist you when your own words won't come.

INTRODUCTION

I pray right now as you read that you will find some comfort and solace in the words I've written within this book; I pray that you will be encouraged to seek whatever help you may need to make it through your cloudy days; most of all, I pray you keep moving forward, knowing that healing is a process and that you can take one tiny step in that direction today (you've picked up this book!). I pray God reveals His strength to you this day and provides exactly what you need.

If you are ever feeling like you cannot go on, I ask that you call this number immediately: 1-800-273-8255 or dial 988; you don't have to suffer alone so keep this number nearby and use it if you need it.

CRY OUT

Matthew 27:45–50

About three in the afternoon Jesus cried out in a loud voice, "Eli, Eli, lema sabachthani?" (which means "My God, my God, why have you forsaken me?").
MATTHEW 27:46

Depression is complicated, to say the least. The numbness, lethargy, disinterest, and sadness often cannot be understood by anyone who has not experienced the complicated illness.

And what about faith? Where is it during these very low points in our lives? That's a question those who love us dearly yet have not experienced depression may pose too. (They just don't understand why you can't shake this or snap out of it.)

Faith and depression can exist in the same space. Just because you're walking through a low point doesn't mean you do not have faith. Even Jesus suffered mightily and questioned God. Depression can make you do that.

But Jesus, the Master Teacher, continues to enlighten us through His example. His words uttered while on the cross teach us to cry out to God especially when we're in excruciating pain. As Jesus moved closer to His ultimate mission on earth, He cried out to His Father, God. Jesus stared death in the face as He was drawn up on a cross. He understood what was about to happen as a part of His purpose, His mission, yet He cried out: "Father, why have you forsaken me?" (see Matthew 27:46).

Can't you hear the agony in those words? Jesus feels abandoned by His Father—but I've never heard anyone question Jesus's faith. The very fact that He is crying out to God means

Jesus acknowledges God and His control over everything. Crying out can serve as a means to release your agony and acknowledge that God is still God—even in the midst of your pain.

Crying out during bouts of depression may not ease the pain immediately, but it's a model from Jesus that we can follow. And it may just draw us closer to our God—which in the end is a win. Crying out like Jesus may be the reminder you need to know that you are going to be okay.

MY CONFESSION

I can cry out. I can yell at God—even question God—as uninvited pain takes up residence in my body and mind. I have no answers, but I do have the ability to cry and lament and the assurance that God hears, sees, and cares for me.

If Jesus cried out, so can you. Release what's on your heart to God.

PROGRESS, NOT PERFECTION

Take a few moments and cry out to God. Share what's on your heart and mind, how you feel, what concerns you. Release your thoughts to your Father who cares for you (see 1 Peter 5:7).

My God, my God: Sometimes I feel forsaken. Why am I enduring so much pain that I cannot always explain it to others? Help me. Be with me. Hear my prayer. Amen.

DOWNCAST SⵔUL
Psalm 42:1–5

*My tears have been my food day and night, while people
say to me all day long, "Where is your God?"*
PSALM 42:3

If you think you may be depressed but are conflicted about how
a person of faith can be depressed, it may be helpful to remind
yourself of biblical people of faith who also dealt with depression. It may have been called something else—or not diagnosed
at all—but a careful look at Scripture shows the likes of David,
Elijah, and even Jesus dealing with what we might call depression today. And we can learn from these biblical giants and others how to navigate our blues.

In today's passage, the writer of this psalm—evidently a worship leader—is crying out and asking, Why is his soul so downcast, why are his tears so constant, like food, in the day and the
night? The psalmist is clearly disturbed within. He recalls how
he used to gleefully and cheerfully go to God's house, leading a
processional with instruments of praise. The writer recalls being
joyful when worshipping God and getting chances to enter into
His house and presence.

But something has shifted. The psalmist no longer feels like
his former self. He no longer wants to enter into God's house
with joy and praise.

But in the midst of the psalmist's lament (which can help the
soul; cry out!), he offers the prescription he needs. He tells himself to put his hope in God, to praise God, and to remember all
He has done in the past.

This is a good formula for when we are downcast and depressed and perhaps may not feel the connection to God or others we once enjoyed. We can lament (cry out and share our emotions: grieve, mourn, complain, release), but we can also talk to ourselves like the psalmist does and remind ourselves to put our hope in God. Why? We can list all of the ways He has helped us in the past. And hopefully soon we too will be, like the downcast psalm writer, praising God again.

MY CONFESSION

I know God is present even when I may not feel God's presence. *You can cry out to God when your soul is downcast.*

PROGRESS, NOT PERFECTION

Make a list of things God has done for you in the past. How can this list give your downcast soul hope?

God of hope: I need you to lift up my downcast soul. Help me to recall the ways you've brought me through in the past as I lean on you for strength to make it today. Amen.

WHEN WE ARE DISTRESSED, PART I

1 Kings 19:1–9

He himself went a day's journey into the wilderness. He came to a broom bush, sat down under it and prayed that he might die. "I have had enough, LORD," he said. "Take my life; I am no better than my ancestors." Then he lay down under the bush and fell asleep. All at once an angel touched him and said, "Get up and eat." He looked around, and there by his head was some bread baked over hot coals, and a jar of water. He ate and drank and then lay down again.

1 KINGS 19:4-6

Elijah is another biblical figure many admire and consider to be a mighty, faithful man. Yet, when I read Elijah's story, I see more. I definitely see a courageous prophet who stood up to King Ahab and his wife, Jezebel. But I also see a human being grappling with issues of fatigue that led to depression.

Elijah shows us some important ways to deal (and not deal) with our blues.

In the first part of 1 Kings 19, Elijah was scared even though he had just defeated many of his enemies. With God's help, he had performed the miraculous. (Elijah had just challenged the people who worshipped an idol god to have their idol send fire; when their god could not deliver their request, Elijah demonstrated the one and only God's power to send the fire. See 1 Kings 18:16–39.) Yet when we see him in today's Scripture,

Elijah is telling God to take his life. He is ready to die because he has had enough. Elijah feels like a failure.

In this passage of Scripture, we have some prescriptions to assist with the overwhelming symptoms of the blues, severe fatigue, and depression.

1. Go to sleep. Get your rest. Take a nap; sleep in; go to bed earlier. However you can manage to get more rest, do it. If you had a cold or another type of illness, you'd rest. Don't think any differently about emotional illnesses. You need your rest—sometimes more rest than you would normally.

2. Eat. And eat foods that will help you. It has been shown that processed foods and fast foods (fried items) can enhance depressed moods. As best as you can, try to leave those alone during this time. Use food as another form of treatment and medicine. Find foods that can help your mood—fresh fruits and vegetables; good, lean meat (if you eat meat). Ask someone you trust to prepare a few meals—many who might want to help don't know how. You can give them some suggestions.

3. Pray. Even when it feels like God doesn't hear you, know that God does. That's what Elijah did when he cried out to God and asked for God to take his life. He was praying. And God answered with some help through an angel's message.

What will you do today to practice one or more of Elijah's prescriptions for depression?

MY CONFESSION

I can rest, eat well, and pray today no matter how I feel.

If you are considering harming yourself, know that there is help. Reach out at 1-800-273-8255 or dial 988.

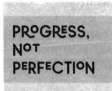

PROGRESS, NOT PERFECTION

Follow Elijah's prescription today. How will you get more rest, eat better, and remember to pray?

My God, my God: I need you today. Give me what I need to make it through this day and through this season of distress. Help me to rest, choose good food, and keep praying. Send me the help I need. Amen.

4

WHEN WE ARE DISTRESSED, PART 2

1 Kings 19:9–18

Yet I reserve seven thousand in Israel—all whose knees have not bowed down to Baal and whose mouths have not kissed him.

1 KINGS 19:18

Depression can make you exaggerate everything. Getting dressed feels like a monumental undertaking. Just thinking about going to an outing can feel like the most wearisome task ever. *I have nothing to wear, I won't know anyone (although someone had to invite me), I won't talk to anyone, I won't like anything or anyone there.* The smallest of issues can turn into huge, catastrophic events—all before they leave our mind. That's exaggeration.

Look at Elijah again today. This man of God was suffering from severe burnout and exhaustion from his zealous work. He thought no one—no one—was on his side, the side of the Lord (1 Kings 19:14). Yet, God told him He had reserved seven thousand in Israel who had not turned to the idol Baal. There were at least seven thousand people on the right side of the issue, yet Elijah felt he was the only one who had remained faithful.

I get it. When you don't feel well, you think everything is crumbling around you. You feel alone and desperate and exhausted and burned out. You're tired of the work. You're tired of the fight. You, like Elijah, may just want to give up. (Remember, if you're having suicidal thoughts—you think about harming yourself—please call 1-800-273-8255 or dial 988.)

I tell myself *not* to make decisions when I'm feeling like

Elijah. I know I'm not thinking straight and everything seems exaggerated. So, I wait. I don't make big decisions until I'm better—that way things won't seem too big or overwhelming and I won't feel like my back is up against the wall when it just may not be.

Get some rest. Wait to hear from God; He just may let you know that things are not as dire as they seem. There may be more people on your side than you know. There may be some resources right there in plain sight that will be revealed to you. Just keep going. Keep looking and listening for God.

MY CONFESSION

I will not make any major decisions when I do not feel well. *When you're depressed, everything seems too big, too hard to tackle. Take a rest and wait.*

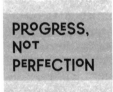

PROGRESS, NOT PERFECTION

Write about what feels overwhelming for you today. Can it wait? If you have to finish today, how can you break it up into smaller, manageable tasks?

Faithful God: I admit I sometimes feel like everything is just too big and too hard to handle. I feel like Elijah and I just want to give up. Give me strength, wisdom, and clarity to know what needs to be done now and what can wait as I wait for your healing touch. Amen.

5

HELP FOR ANXIETY
Philippians 4:4–8

Do not be anxious about anything, but in every situation, by prayer and petition, with thanksgiving, present your requests to God. And the peace of God, which transcends all understanding, will guard your hearts and your minds in Christ Jesus.
PHILIPPIANS 4:6–7

Anxiety—the feeling of overwhelming anxiousness or panic—can come in many different forms and produce different outcomes. It can paralyze us and make us fearful of situations that may or may not ever occur. Anxiety can look like nervous energy, unsettled spirits, impatience, and being overly concerned.

Wringing the hands—or just an unsettled heart—can be a sign of anxiety. I'm not sure if Paul ever dealt with anxiety, but he does provide us a solution for the anxious feelings we may experience throughout life.

He says specifically to not be anxious about anything—our future, our concerns, our habits. Nothing. When anxiety comes, we can do as Paul suggests: pray. And he says to pray with thanksgiving, remembering all we have to be thankful for. Paul's prescription forces our minds off of our concerns and shifts them to our blessings. It's a mind change—an intentional decision to focus on what God has done for us.

Try it. And watch the anxiety flee as you thank God. Watch your list of thanksgiving grow as you rattle off another thing to be grateful for. And like with any good medicine, you can expect relief—in the form of peace. But this is no ordinary peace. It's the peace of God that transcends our understanding.

No, your situation may not change instantly, but you can change and allow peace and gratitude to calm your nerves and shift your focus.

MY CONFESSION

I will be anxious for nothing.

Consistent gratefulness through prayer is a cure for anxiety.

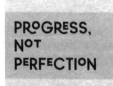
PROGRESS, NOT PERFECTION

Start a gratitude list. Write out as many things as you can think of to be grateful for this day. Craft them into a prayer and repeat them as often as needed.

Dear Lord: I want to be anxious for nothing. I submit my worries to you, and I shift my focus to thanking you for so many things. I want to thank you for _____,

_____, _____, _____

[keep going!]. Amen.

THE POWER OF MUSIC
Psalm 147:1–7

Sing to the LORD with grateful praise;
make music to our God on the harp.
PSALM 147:7

A song can change the atmosphere. It can change your mood and mind too—even if just for a moment.

What songs lift you up? What lyrics take you back to a joyful moment or memory? What words remind you of God's faithfulness, salvation, and characteristics? These are the songs that can help you on a difficult day.

Even when you don't feel like it, pump that song up—loud. Hit replay. Move your mouth to the words and allow them to seep into your heart and shift your mood and mind.

The feeling of relief your favorite tune brings may not last long—or cure what ails you—but there's nothing wrong with playing it again and again, using the lyrics to remind you of what you know deep down even when you don't feel them.

And while you're at it, if you can, move a bit to the beat of your song. Movement can't hurt either.

Do it and sing to the Lord with praise—rattling off what you have to be grateful for, thanking God for healing and restoration, thanking Him for even this moment regardless of how difficult it seems. Make music to God through your favorite song. And hit repeat.

MY CONFESSION

I will allow a song to soothe my soul this day as I make music to God.

Music can change the atmosphere and your mood.

....

Create a list of songs that can lift your mood. Keep that playlist handy. Some of my favorite artists include Mary Mary, Tamela Mann, and Kirk Franklin.

....

Dear Lord: Thank you for the gift of music and its increased availability to me. Give me the strength to press play and repeat throughout the day as I make music to you, seeking to lift my mood and think of your faithfulness. Amen.

A WAY TO BLESS OTHERS

2 Corinthians 1:3–7

*[God] comforts us in all our troubles, so that we can
comfort those in any trouble with the comfort
we ourselves receive from God.*
2 CORINTHIANS 1:4

While we're on music and its power to heal and lift our spirits during times we feel blue, let's not forget the entire genre of music so appropriately named the blues, which was created by Black people working on plantations to express their sadness. From the sorrows and pains of life—trying to make it in a land of segregation, economic upheaval, tumultuous interpersonal relationships fractured even more by the stress and haunting trauma of the past and present—comes music, an expression of the pain and sorrow that can move a people to sway and nod their heads. It has the ability to connect with your emotions and transport you to another place or give you enough umph to keep moving to the next day. It's how many survived awful conditions, awaiting the moment they could get away and listen to story in music; it's how "big mama" and some who weren't afraid to mix a little secular and holy got through cleaning houses, chopping cotton, and doing many other undesirable chores. This music carried them through. The blues sustained a people from week to week and created careers for many with a steel guitar, a microphone, or a harmonica.

As you walk through your cloudy days, think of the contributions of those who expressed themselves through troubles.

Consider how they utilized their pain to produce something beautiful. While I'm not sure what they felt during this time, I do know what they left behind even in the midst of their pain.

Sometimes finding the creative outlet for the blues is about more than you; it's about the legacy you will leave too. If you don't want to push forward for yourself, you can push forward for those coming behind you. What contributions are you making and leaving for others? How will life be better because you passed through this world? What is your legacy? Even if you can't think of answers to these questions, consider the legacy of the men and women who droned out their problems, created rhythms, and shared the emotions bottled in their hearts with the world. They left a genre of music whose chords and beats trickled into gospel music and more. Their pain produced more than agony and hurt; their emotions fueled a creativity they could not begin to imagine.

In addition to music, we've also received literature, visual art, and more from the expression of folks suffering with the blues. There just may be an outlet for you to express what you're experiencing, and this outlet can bless many; you can be a blessing to others.

Dare to think about the future; dare to see your contributions—beyond what you feel right now.

MY CONFESSION
I will look for a good way to express myself when I am down.
Your emotions can fuel creativity that you can't even imagine.

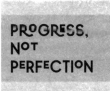

PROGRESS, NOT PERFECTION

Tap into the creative side of your brain and try expressing your grief through writing, music, art, photography, and so on.

Creator Lord: Show me how to express myself even while I walk through cloudy days. Thank you for those who have gone before me and created wonderful works of art, even through their blues. Amen.

PRECIOUS LORD

Psalm 23

Even though I walk through the darkest valley, I will fear no evil, for you are with me; your rod and your staff, they comfort me.
PSALM 23:4

One of my favorite stories of how creative expression from pain has blessed and comforted so many is the story of Thomas Dorsey's writing of the touching hymn "Precious Lord." As the story is told, Dorsey, who is known as the "Father of Gospel Music," received a telegram immediately after he sat down after singing several songs in a hot church in St. Louis. Dorsey had traveled to the city from his home in Chicago reluctantly because his wife was in her final month of pregnancy; however, he recalled that many people were expecting him in St. Louis. So, after he fulfilled his promise of singing at the church, a young messenger gave him the telegram that read: Your wife just died.

Filled with sorrow and many questions, Dorsey returned to Chicago, where he discovered that his wife had died while giving birth to their son. According to the United Methodist Church Discipleship Ministries, Dorsey said he swung between "grief and joy." His wife was dead. He had a newborn son. However, his son's health took a turn too, and by that night he also died. Dorsey buried his wife, Nettie, and their little son together in the same casket.

Dorsey was submerged in grief. He said, "I felt that God had done me an injustice. I didn't want to serve Him any more or write gospel songs. I just wanted to go back to that jazz world I once knew so well."

Still, a good friend knew what Dorsey needed and took him to a neighborhood music school. It was there, in the quiet room, Dorsey sat at a piano and poured out his heart to God. The result: the stirring words of the beautiful hymn that's been sung in at least forty different languages.

This beloved hymn would go on to minister to many people and even become a sort of anthem sung at many rallies during the Civil Rights Movement.

MY CONFESSION

I will cry out to God in my grief and pain.

From his pain, Dorsey poured out his heart and wrote "Precious Lord."

PROGRESS, NOT PERFECTION

Listen to "Precious Lord" by Thomas Dorsey.

Precious Lord: Please take my hand and guide me through my cloudy days. I trust you are by my side and can help me navigate through all I encounter. Amen.

A REFUGE

Nahum 1:1–8

The LORD is good, a refuge in times of trouble.
He cares for those who trust in him.

NAHUM 1:7

What does a refuge look like? I see a shelter in the midst of rain or a storm, or perhaps a bunker or fort on the battlefield.

I'm not sure we use *refuge* as a part of everyday language anymore, but it helps to say the word and see God as a refuge, a place of safety, a respite in the midst of the turmoil and storm. In today's Scripture, we find a passage in the middle of turmoil and punishment. It's a message to Israel's dangerous enemy Nineveh, but it's also a reminder of one of God's comforting characteristics and just who He is: a refuge in times of trouble.

Today—regardless of how you are feeling—ask God to be your refuge. Ask God to provide some comfort as your refuge, some shelter, some protection as you navigate your sea of emotions.

Each time sadness or pain or hopelessness creeps up, whisper a prayer to your Refuge.

Use the word *refuge* to describe God as you pray and cry out.

If you journal, write what that word means to you. Perhaps find a song describing God as a refuge. Create a picture or find an image that reminds you of God as a refuge . . . and rest in that one portion of God's personality.

Seek refuge in God; allow God to be your protection and shelter in the midst of your storm this day.

MY CONFESSION

I will seek help from God, my refuge, today.

God is an ever-present help, your refuge in time of need. Keep seeking your Refuge until you feel peace—and thereafter.

PROGRESS, NOT PERFECTION

Write down what it means to have God as your refuge. Use lots of descriptive words and think about them throughout the day.

God, my refuge: Thank you for loving me so much that you want to protect me and keep me in the times of trouble. Help me to see you as my refuge this day. Help me to run and hide in the truth of your presence. Amen.

LESSONS FROM MY DEPRESSION

James 1:2–4

Consider it pure joy, my brothers and sisters,
whenever you face trials of many kinds.
JAMES 1:2

I think it's safe to say on these pages: I hate depression. I absolutely hate how it makes me feel—numb, unmotivated, and tired. I've been in meetings discussing things I know I love (like Black women and the Bible) and what did I do? Scoff down M&M's. It was my coping mechanism, but I knew something was severely wrong because I was just there, not really *present*; I couldn't get excited about something near and dear to my heart. The perfect project for me to work on was merely "something I had to do."

I probably experienced my longest bout of depression several years ago. I always get anxious when I think signs are popping up again (I want to sleep longer than normal; I want to scoff down chocolate because I don't feel like doing anything else).

But one day it occurred to me, What if depression can be seen as a marker for me to draw closer to God? What if those times I spent depressed actually made me grow stronger? I know, for sure, they've given me special compassion for people who are not feeling their best. Through my bouts of depression, my ordinarily goal-achieving self realized that sometimes you just can't do it. Sometimes getting out of bed is the win. I don't know if I would have ever come to this conclusion if I hadn't experienced depression firsthand.

Because of my depression, I sincerely relate to people differently. I can count it joy that I experienced (and experience) the trial of depression because I am growing, maturing, becoming more completely the person God has designed me to be. Look at that, depression. I am not defeated. I am stronger.

MY CONFESSION

My trials may be bringing me closer to maturity in Christ.
Even though depression doesn't feel good, it can produce something good. Depression, anxiety, or blues can be a period of growth and maturity.

PROGRESS, NOT PERFECTION

Think ahead. What can you see differently since you've experienced the blues? How will you respond to others going through difficult periods?

Amazing Lord: Thank you for the reminder that you may be producing something powerful within me even as I go through this blue season. Give me what I need and help me to remember what I am learning, to reach others. Amen.

MORE LESSONS FROM MY DEPRESSION

Romans 8:18–30

And we know that in all things God works for the good of those who love him, who have been called according to his purpose. For those God foreknew he also predestined to be conformed to the image of his Son, that he might be the firstborn among many brothers and sisters. And those he predestined, he also called; those he called, he also justified; those he justified, he also glorified.

ROMANS 8:28–30

After a relatively deep conversation with a friend, she paused and said, "Katara, you've grown so much." There's nothing like someone from your inner circle remarking on your growth. She had heard my cries. She had been a firsthand witness of a low period in my life and now she was reflecting on what she saw as growth. I thanked her for her observation and quickly commented more to myself than her: "This is the result of three years of therapy, hard work, and prayer."

In the midst of those very difficult three years—and probably even more than that because it often takes time to actually make the moves needed to seek healing—I prayed and talked about some issues bothering me. Why did I react the way I did? Why did I allow some people in my life, knowing they didn't mean me any good? Why didn't I speak up earlier? How did I see myself? What caused me to see myself that way? Yes, those are some deep questions. And may I suggest, if you're going to dive into uncovering answers for yourself, that you surround yourself with those who love you unconditionally and those who are cheering for you to be whole and healthy (that's not everyone in your circle!).

But what I've learned from that dark time in my life and the eventual fruit of those hard days, and of answering those hard questions, is that I was being formed into a new creation. God was taking things and working them together for my good, just as Paul describes in Romans 8. Those days definitely didn't always feel good. I didn't always like the answers I came up with. And I am continually working on me and how to forgo repeating some of those patterns that caused me to suppress feelings and eventually become depressed. But as I look back, I can see how those days formed me into the new person I am today. In my new phases of life, I lean on what I learned during those days. I can recognize warning signs and I can most times seek out the help I need before darkness takes over. But I've also reminded myself that I've come through the dark before so, if I enter again, I can trust and believe that God has a way out for me again. I'm not as scared of darkness as I once was. I know firsthand the light is a-coming.

I'm thankful God knows who I am and who He has called me to be—and I'm certain He predestined me to be a reminder to you that depression doesn't last always and that depression can render some valuable lessons that shape and transform us into the people we are designed to be.

MY CONFESSION

Even during my dark days, God is working to shape me into the person He wants me to become.

All things work together for good for those of us who love God.

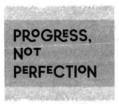

PROGRESS, NOT PERFECTION

What hard questions do you want to answer during your dark days?

God of all: I proclaim that all things work together for good because I love you. I know every step isn't easy and won't be good, but I believe you have the ability to form good from the difficult parts of my life. I await to see your light. Amen.

12

IN TIMES OF GRIEF
Matthew 5:3–10

Blessed are those who mourn, for they will be comforted.
MATTHEW 5:4

Some of the darkest days I've experienced occurred after I had to say goodbye to my mother due to her death at age sixty-three. No one wants to lose a loved one at any age, but sixty-three seemed really young to me. I knew so many vibrant and seemingly healthy people who were well beyond that age.

As a Christian—and because my mother was my first and best Christian role model—I didn't expect her death to hit me nearly as hard as it did. After all, hadn't she been living for this day? She had proclaimed her trust and belief in Jesus at a young age and had lived out her life accordingly. I was certain she had a future with an eternal life. So why was I so broken? Why did I find it difficult to do some of the simple things in life after her death?

One of my breakthrough moments came when I was in a therapy session. (Thankfully, I had been seeing a therapist for a year or so before my mom's death to deal with depression brought on by other life events.) As I spoke with my beloved therapist, I ran through several reasons why I hadn't been able to have a good cry about my mom's death. I'm normally not one to hold on to tears—I was known as a crybaby as a kid—but somehow I hadn't shed many tears around Mom's death. As we unpacked my why, I told my therapist I always got headaches after crying really hard, and I had too much to do to stop for a headache. I continued to list all of the "important" things I had to do. I can still see my therapist's face, blankly staring at me, awaiting me to catch up and reflect on the words I had just said. I was too busy to cry. I was too busy to grieve my mother's death, the death of the woman who first showed me unconditional love, the woman I had known was right by my side for nearly thirty-five years, my biggest supporter and cheerleader, my guide, my prayer warrior, and teacher. I did not have the time to grieve a significant loss? Girl, please!

If I could go back and talk to that young woman in the midst of life-changing mourning, who'd just planned and participated in a beautiful celebration of the life of such a meaningful and pivotal relationship, I'd ask: Girl, what you got to do that's so important? Apparently, I was consumed with my to-do list and I had lost sight of the reality that I was no good until I took care of my emotions. I could keep running and pretending like I had no time because of work, friends, community, and church work (yep, you know we can use even "good" things to mask what needs to be taken care of), but my grief would still be there, waiting for me to acknowledge it, waiting for me to cry so I could begin to heal, waiting for me to receive the comfort God offers to us. Dare I say, either you grieve now or you grieve later—but, sis, it will come out, one way or the other.

MY CONFESSION

I will take the time to mourn what I grieve.

Comfort awaits those who mourn.

....

PROGRESS, NOT PERFECTION

What have you not grieved? How can you release your emotions and receive comfort?

....

NAVIGATING THE BLUES

God of comfort: I know you've promised to comfort me when I mourn. Help me to release feelings of loss and allow you to provide what I need to heal. Thank you for being right by my side throughout my days of grief. Amen.

HOLIDAYS AND THE BLUES
Proverbs 4:10–14

*Hold on to instruction, do not let it go; guard it well,
for it is your life.*
PROVERBS 4:13

Well, another thing I've learned about dealing with grief is that it can seep in at any time and overwhelm you. I think this is especially true on holidays and at special times, and even other times that are also filled with joy. At the birth of my child, I cried with excitement and all the hope and promise a newborn ushers into the world, but I also felt a hole, an emptiness, a sadness of knowing my mother was not present with me physically in this moment.

During an earlier time, when I closed on a condo, I received the keys early, a few hours before the official closing because I lived in the building already and the deal had gone through pretty smoothly. When I walked in the new apartment to do my own little walkthrough before going to the title office to sign all of those papers, I saw the larger apartment space I was blessed to purchase. I recalled how much fun my mother had decorating my sister's home, and I immediately collapsed to the floor in grief. I was alone in my new place, and I was filled with sadness, suddenly and shockingly. Who expects to grieve when purchasing a home? It took me nearly an hour to compose myself and get dressed to go to the title office. (Imagine my attorney's fear as he and others kept calling my cell phone!) I had no intentions of needing an hour to compose myself; I had no intentions of even crying when I entered the apartment; I was going to check in on those last-minute repairs, give God a praise, and head on to the title office. But grief can sneak up on you unexpectedly.

Know that lurking feeling can come during the holidays too; all of the holidays I celebrated with Mom are different today. We have an empty seat at the table—even as we've expanded the table with new family members and loved ones. In this case, I tell myself it is okay to have new traditions. It's okay to take a trip during the holidays and see my family at other moments. Or, it's okay to give myself a moment to take a walk outside and clear my head and release emotions. It is different and I don't need to pretend that things are the same—that can only add more stress to my life.

I also recognize that many others deal with stress and the blues during the holidays, because of complicated family structures. Perhaps you have not-so-fond memories of encounters with those you feel forced to eat with. Give yourself the permission to find the family that brings you joy—which can be the friends you have, the family you have chosen.

When your well-being can become more important to you than your traditions, you will become more able to celebrate in a new, healthier way—and you will be even more empowered to deal with seasonal holiday blues.

MY CONFESSION

I will press through the holidays and special occasions.

Grief can seep in and overwhelm you.

PROGRESS, NOT PERFECTION

During the next holiday, allow wisdom to guide your plans, not traditions.

HOLIDAYS AND THE BLUES

My God: Give me the courage I need to make changes for my well-being around traditions I've held for so long. Show me the importance of caring for myself. Amen.

ANOTHER TYPE OF GRIEF

Matthew 6:14–15

But if you do not forgive others their sins,
your Father will not forgive your sins.
MATTHEW 6:15

As I've looked back over my life and my bouts of depression, I've realized there's something else that contributed to my blues. And when left unaddressed—or dare I say untreated—that feeling can grow and produce more harm than I ever imagined. Now I'm not saying every episode of depression has a direct correlation to an emotion or incident. Sometimes it is genetic or based on hormones or something we cannot explain. But sometimes, if we're honest, loss can cause our depression. I talked about the grief of losing my mother earlier, but in the midst of that mourning period, I realized I had also lost a dream. I was grieving an opportunity I thought would flourish into one of my life's dreams, but instead it had not and had left me feeling lost and with little hope. My next move was unknown and this was tough to handle.

What does Langston Hughes write about in "Harlem," sometimes also referred to as "A Dream Deferred"? He asks what happens to a dream that isn't fulfilled. He lists several questions about the possibilities of having a dream that doesn't come to fruition. I'd add to the prolific writer's questions: Does the dream that doesn't happen cause resentment, pain, depression—by-products of something that was once a beautiful desire but that has waned and not been achieved?

Whether this type of grief is brought on by a lost relationship (romantic or even platonic), a missed opportunity like mine, or even the loss of a job, it can cause you to sink into a low place, especially if it is not dealt with.

For me, releasing what wasn't meant to be is a tough process, especially when I've fantasized about it and created a full-blown script in my head. But forgiveness, a process I've grown to call cyclical, has helped. I need help letting go of what I once thought would come to pass. I know I need God to forgive me for sins in my life, so I too need to forgive those who stopped my realization of opportunities, including myself for the role I played. Forgiveness is not a quick, one-and-done process; it takes time, intentionality, prayer . . . and the bitter thoughts can sometimes creep back up after you think you've forgiven. But, as I heard and reflected on when visiting Robben Island where Nelson Mandela was held for many years: forgiveness is not for your enemies; it's for you. There's no use in living in prison mentally when you've been set free physically!

MY CONFESSION

I will let go of what I have lost.

What happens to a dream that has not become reality?

....

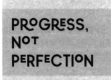

Spend time reflecting on what you have not released or forgiven.

....

God of forgiveness: Give me what I need to release my disappointments and losses to you. Give me the strength and willingness to forgive so that I may be free and open to your forgiveness. Amen.

WHAT TO DO WITH WORRY
Matthew 6:25–34

Can any one of you by worrying add a single hour to your life?
MATTHEW 6:27

If you're anything like me, when you are suffering with the blues, anxiety, or full-on depression, life seems overwhelming. Your to-do list (if you can manage to keep one) is never-ending and you don't have the strength to tackle anything on it. All of it seems like too much. You're not interested in doing even what under "normal" circumstances would be your favorite, and the stuff you never really wanted to do seems like an albatross tied around your neck, pulling you further down and causing your symptoms to intensify.

I believe a part of navigating through these moments is facing them. Calling them out and saying, "Today, I just don't feel it. So, what do I absolutely need to do today?" Is it making it to work? Is it waking up the kids and giving them cold cereal for breakfast? Lowering your expectations for yourself can help here. Count those tasks as must-dos and use your energy to do them. And the rest? Don't worry about it. It won't get done from worry anyway.

In today's verse, Jesus reminds us that we cannot do anything with worry; it's futile and worthless. We can't add a day to our lives because we are worried. We can't add energy to our life to get those things done because of worry. So let it go; keep your energy for the must-do things on your list and move the other stuff. There will be a day you feel better. Be gentle with yourself. Say a prayer. Take some deep breaths. Close your eyes and repeat

Jesus's words from today's Scripture. Take this day one moment at a time and leave the worry behind. Pray for your daily bread, what you need this day. And don't worry about tomorrow.

If your down feelings continue for a prolonged amount of time—where you actually can't do your work or finish anything—it may be time to consider seeking professional help. I've done it and it is liberating to share what's happening in the mind. I didn't even realize some of those thoughts were adding to my depression. There's help for what ails you, trust me.

MY CONFESSION

Some days, I just don't feel like doing much. On those days, I'll give myself a break and not worry.

Sometimes focusing on what absolutely has to be done is enough. When you're in a depressed state, you need to give yourself extra grace.

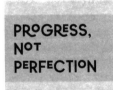

PROGRESS, NOT PERFECTION

Pull out your to-do list and circle only two or three things that need to be done today. Don't worry about the other stuff.

God of love: Help me to be gentle with myself today. Remind me of your love and grace and help me extend love and grace to myself. Amen.

A CHEERFUL HEART

Proverbs 17:22, 24

A cheerful heart is good medicine,
but a crushed spirit dries up the bones.
PROVERBS 17:22

Another method I use to deal with the overwhelming feeling of the blues is to keep a list of the things I enjoy. I try to make this list when I'm not overwhelmed or feeling anxious; actually, it's a good idea to create the list as you find yourself enjoying activities. Write down enjoyable activities so when you're not feeling well you don't have to search for what might lift your mood. You can take out your handy list and perhaps try something that normally makes you feel good. Waiting until you need the pick-me-up to think of the activity usually doesn't work—you're not at your best and you're not thinking as smoothly as you normally do.

Some of the items on my list include reading a good fiction book, a walk outside on a nice day, a Zumba class, baking, watching one of my favorite movies (comedies work best for me), using my inspiration playlist, or listening to an album with lots of songs that I love.

Make your own list and add anything that makes your heart cheerful. After all, that is some good and natural medicine, as Proverbs clearly states. We take medicine to make us feel better when we have a headache or some other ailment. Adding the medicine of a cheerful heart is as important. Increase the "dosage" when you need to and look for your spirit to be elevated.

Look for what makes your heart glad and cheerful and take

in more of it. Keep track of what gives you a boost and a smile. Do those things as often as needed. "Rinse and repeat" is a good motto for anything that makes your heart cheerful. It's wise to keep those things handy and on autopilot for days when you need the extra lift.

MY CONFESSION
I will learn what makes my heart sing.
Do what makes you happy.

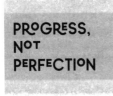

PROGRESS, NOT PERFECTION

Start your list. What makes your heart sing? Add to your list as you discover more activities that bring you happiness. There's no limit to how long your list can be. Keep it handy.

All-knowing and all-seeing God: Thank you for creating activities that make my heart sing. Remind me of what gives me joy and help me to participate in those activities as often as possible. Amen.

BE GENTLE WITH YOURSELF
1 Corinthians 13:4–8

*Love is patient, love is kind. It does not envy,
it does not boast, it is not proud. It does not dishonor
others, it is not self-seeking, it is not easily angered,
it keeps no record of wrongs.*
1 CORINTHIANS 13:4–5

Many Christians have heard the beautiful language of 1 Corinthians 13, also known as the Love Chapter. It is often quoted at weddings and lifted up in sermons as the esteemed way to love one another.

But, have you ever used these words to think more about how you are to love yourself? After all, a part of the greatest commandment reminds us to love others as we love ourselves (Matthew 22:37–39). How would your language about yourself change if you were patient with yourself? How would you treat yourself differently if you were kind to yourself? How would the voice inside of your head be different if you reminded yourself that love for yourself is not easily angered or disappointed or doesn't rehearse wrongs?

I bet you'd treat yourself differently if you turned a mirror around on the Love Chapter and remembered that to love this way is applicable not only to our neighbors but to ourselves.

When you're in the midst of the blues or full-on depression, it is tempting to be hard on yourself and think negatively about yourself. Today, I challenge you to use the words in 1 Corinthians 13 to love yourself better, to give yourself a break, because love always hopes, protects, trusts, and perseveres. Because you love yourself, you can keep going, looking for and expecting a better day. Be gentle with yourself. Be loving toward yourself.

MY CONFESSION

I can love myself well.

Be patient and kind with yourself.

Journal about ways you can love yourself like 1 Corinthians 13 describes.

God of love: I know you love me—as evidenced by your gift of Christ. Now, teach me to love myself and to treat myself well as I heal and continue to grow into the person you've called me to be. Amen.

ALSO, BE KIND TO YOURSELF

Proverbs 18:20–21

*The tongue has the power of life and death,
and those who love it will eat its fruit.*

PROVERBS 18:21

I'll start off with a command: Don't beat yourself up! I mean it and I'm talking to you.

I share this message with friends all of the time because a dear friend has encouraged me with the words of being gentle to myself. None of us would sit around and let a friend talk to herself like this: *I am a failure, I can do nothing right, I've failed again.* None of us would let someone talk to our child—or any child—like that. None of us would let someone say that about our loved ones. It's just not productive language. And most of us, despite the circumstances, can find something nice to say about someone in any situation.

But, what happens when it is internal language? What happens when you are the one who needs encouraging? You'll need to find the honesty to say, *I'm not going to beat myself up. I'm going to cancel those negative thoughts and remind myself of who I am, who created me, who saved me.*

We know the power our tongues have; we know the power our thoughts have. When you're down and depressed, it's no time to turn on yourself and start using your words against yourself. You need every encouraging word possible to keep you going on this journey. Stop and reframe your thoughts and words. Be kind to yourself.

In the midst of my struggles, I have to remind myself: *I'm more than my last project. I'm much greater than my last task. I'm bigger than even this depressed state I find myself in. I'm not thinking straight now, so I'm just not going to think. I'm going to do what needs to be done (whatever that is) and I'm going to rest. I'm going to wait. I'm going to pray. I'm going to hope for the moment when my sanity returns, and I can think straight and encourage myself. But what I'm not going to do is beat myself up. Nope. Not me. Not today. I am not going to talk to myself like that.*

Will you join me in the quest to treat yourself better? To at the very least not allow those thoughts and words to trip you up and make you feel bad?

MY CONFESSION

I will use my tongue to uplift myself, not hurt myself.

We know words have power.

....

Reframe every negative word or thought that creeps into your mind today.

....

My Creator: I know you've created me and I know you know exactly what I need today. Help me treat myself well as your child. Amen.

ISOLATION

Hebrews 10:23–25

And let us consider how we may spur one another on toward love and good deeds, not giving up meeting together, as some are in the habit of doing, but encouraging one another—and all the more as you see the Day approaching.

HEBREWS 10:24–25

I recall a specific instance when I was pretty down and out. I believe I was still in the thick of grief from my mother's death. I was invited to a friend's baby shower. Now, I did not feel like attending, but I "tricked" myself into going (I made it easier to attend). The shower was on a Sunday and my friend's home was about twenty minutes away from my church and about thirty-five minutes away from my home. So, on that day, I chose to attend the church service that was closest to the time of the shower, to make it easier to drive to the event because it was closer to the church than my home was. I knew if I attended church during the early service, I'd come back home and perhaps not go to the shower.

So I pushed my way to service; that often lifted my spirits too. And then I pushed my way to the shower that was attended by several good friends. We played games, ate good food, fellowshipped, and prayed for my friend's safe delivery of her baby.

As I drove away, I reflected on how much fun I had. I've always been a game person and I enjoyed seeing my friends. I didn't want to go earlier that morning, but I'm glad I did. That friend's daughter recently turned fifteen. Every time I see her, I smile and reflect on the choice I made to attend her shower.

Tricking ourselves to make appointments and gatherings can be helpful when all we really want to do is pull the cover over our heads. However, we all know that isolation is not what we need during these times. Being around friends can bring much-needed warmth and cheer, and can take our minds off the blues we're feeling. So, what do you need to do to "make" yourself show up to events that you may not feel like attending? Leave extra early to attend to avoid deciding not to go at the last minute? Pack a bag if you're already going to be out so you don't have to return home? Ask a friend to pick you up (or offer to pick one up)?

All of these tricks don't work all of the time, but when you know you'll have a decent time (set the bar low), push yourself to be in fellowship with others. You may feel better when you forgo isolation and enjoy the company of others for a moment.

MY CONFESSION

I will gather with others instead of isolating myself.

Of course you don't feel like going, but push yourself to forgo isolation and engage with people you love and trust.

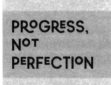

PROGRESS, NOT PERFECTION

Accept an invitation to join some friends for a social event (or create your own invitation). Think of a few tricks to put into place to make sure you get there.

My Lord and my God: Thank you for the company of good friends. I know this life is not meant to be lived in isolation. Give me the extra push I need to engage with others when I don't feel like it. Amen.

A FEW GOOD FRIENDS

Mark 2:1–5

Some men came, bringing to him a paralyzed man, carried by four of them. Since they could not get him to Jesus because of the crowd, they made an opening in the roof above Jesus by digging through it and then lowered the mat the man was lying on. When Jesus saw their faith, he said to the paralyzed man, "Son, your sins are forgiven."

MARK 2:3–5

Let's talk about friends. Sometimes when I'm down, blue, and sad, my friends are the last people I want to tell. I'm known as the positive, encouraging friend. I'm the one others come to for inspiration. But at the very times I need uplifting and inspiration, I often retreat from my loved ones. I decline the calls; I don't accept the invitation. I isolate myself (see the devotion on isolation, page 56).

But today's Scripture reminds me of the beauty of friends. Four friends chose to help their paralyzed friend by lifting him up and carrying him to Jesus. They did what the man couldn't do for himself. They knew how he could be helped. They had faith that Jesus was the answer and they did what was needed to get their friend help.

Oh, the value of a few good friends! Sometimes our help is right there in our friend circle. We have to be vulnerable and trusting enough to let our closest, most valued friends know about our current state of emotions, and we have to let them help us. I know it's not easy, but true friends can help during this time. Whether it's simply a fun time together reminiscing about life, a supportive nudge to call a therapist, or a sweet reminder that God has not left you here on earth to deal with this life alone, friends can be of great value when you're navigating through the blues.

When you are tempted to isolate because of your mood, remember how friends can help at just the right time. Some may be able to do for you what you cannot do for yourself right now. And that's part of what friends are for. Let a few good friends carry you during this time! See their help as extensions of God's provision and God's reminder that you, my sister, are not alone.

MY CONFESSION
I can trust a few friends to help me at times.
I will forgo isolation and share with a trusted friend how I'm truly feeling.

PROGRESS, NOT PERFECTION

Be bold and write out how a friend may be able to help you this week. Then ask for that help.

Merciful Lord: Thank you for those you've put in my life.
Help me to be vulnerable with someone who cares for me.
Amen.

FRIENDS AND WORDS
Job 2:11–13

When Job's three friends, Eliphaz the Temanite, Bildad the Shuhite and Zophar the Naamathite, heard about all the troubles that had come upon him, they set out from their homes and met together by agreement to go and sympathize with him and comfort him.

JOB 2:11

Friends and depression could be an entire chapter in a book. In my case, I've had friends try to cheer me up and make me snap out of it. Friends who've said some pretty insensitive things as they noticed I wasn't really myself. And some friends who've been amazingly supportive—one praying with me to find the right therapist who would respect my faith, or another picking up light-therapy lamps for both of us during this time (see page 102).

While the man in Mark from the previous devotion had supportive friends who did the lifting for him when he could not get to Jesus, sometimes our friends are more like Job's friends. These infamous friends in the book of Job had good intentions, in my opinion. When they heard of the calamity that had befallen their dear friend, they got up and went to his home to comfort him. They wanted to support their friend. But if you're familiar with this story, you'll know that several chapters of the book of Job describe the words these friends spoke, and they came off as downright wrong and insensitive. They blamed Job for his condition; they offered simplistic solutions, telling him to look to God and plead with the Almighty (see Job 8:5)—as if Job hadn't already been talking to God! And they even turned the tables and prioritized their feelings ahead of Job's: "Will your idle talk reduce others to silence?" (11:3). The bottom line: Job's friends were uncomfortable with his situation, and they simply couldn't sit and support him.

That's real. Not every friend is in the position to support you like you need them to on cloudy—or sunny—days.

Instead of sitting with friends like Job's, focus on those God *has* put in a position to help you. Remember, not everyone will be a comfort and helpful in this period of your life. Be thankful for those who are and turn to them.

MY CONFESSION
I will seek out friends who are supportive during this season. *Not every friend will be able to comfort and support you right now.*

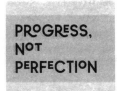

PROGRESS, NOT PERFECTION

List the friends who understand what you're going through and thank God for them today.

God of all: Thank you for friends who can be of comfort to me during dark days. I ask a special blessing on their lives. I also ask that you give me patience and understanding to accept that some friends will not be able to support me right now. Amen.

22

FRIENDS AND MORE WORDS
Jeremiah 29:12–14

Then you will call on me and come and pray to me,
and I will listen to you.
JEREMIAH 29:12

When facing the challenges of a depressed spirit and mind, have you ever been told, "Just pray about it"? I'd definitely list this as another insensitive thing our friends can say to us. Oh, don't get me wrong: as a person of faith, I firmly believe in the power of prayer. I've had prayers answered and I praise God for those answers and try to recall them regularly (although as I age, the list gets too long to recall!). So, naturally, I understand what prayer can do and, more importantly, what the God I pray to can do. But, when I'm in the midst of a depressed moment, to imply that prayer is all I need leads me to think: *You don't think I've taken this condition to God in prayer.* When depression invades your space, trust me, if you're a person of faith, you've prayed about it. You've asked God to get you out of this funk, to lift your mood, and to change the chemicals in your body causing dis-ease. When the numbing impact of the blues hit you, prayer may have been your first point of defense.

However, to say "just pray about it" belittles the condition, in my opinion. After a tough breakup (where I did some pretty dumb things that were outside of my character), I told a friend I was seeking counseling. I wanted to talk through what had happened and get some help processing things so I could move on and become a better person—after all, that's how I normally view a test. My dear friend, who I truly believe had my best interest at heart, told me, "All you need is Jesus and your Bible." I have Jesus, my Bible, prayer—and I still have depression.

Faith can be used as a panacea; it can be flung around in catchy mantras and even quick Bible verses. But those of us who have walked this road trying to navigate the blues know healing sometimes requires more than a Bible verse. Yes, verses can give us hope and inspiration. Yes, prayer can always put us in a better mindset. But what we really need is much more complex than what can be summed up in a quick word. We need it all: everything that will bring us closer to wholeness.

Seek whatever that is for you; seek it faithfully and wholeheartedly, just as you'd seek God. In fact, seek wholeness through your prayers to God and listen for the answers to find steps toward healing.

MY CONFESSION

I will seek God for help and listen for my next step toward healing. *What we really need when dealing with the blues is much more complex than what can be summed up in a quick word.*

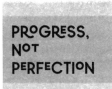

PROGRESS, NOT PERFECTION

List several ways toward wholeness and healing.

Healer God: I know you have the ability to make me whole. I know you can show me tools I need to incorporate to help my healing. Give me the strength and determination to do what needs to be done for my well-being. Thank you for not leaving or forsaking me. Amen.

23

RHYTHM OF UNFORCED GRACE

Matthew 11:25–30

*Are you tired? Worn out? Burned out on religion?
Come to me. Get away with me and you'll recover your life.
I'll show you how to take a real rest. Walk with me and work
with me—watch how I do it. Learn the unforced rhythms of
grace. I won't lay anything heavy or ill-fitting on you. Keep
company with me and you'll learn to live freely and lightly.*

MATTHEW 11:28–30 MSG

One of the many lessons I've learned from praying with a group
of women for the past year—three days a week for an hour—is
to pray using Scripture. This means when we have a prayer request and often sound burdened and worried, the leader of the
prayer call asks: "What Scripture are you standing on?" She asks
the ladies to repeat a Scripture that speaks to their circumstance,
to remind the person in need of what God's Word says about
that situation. That's powerful!

We oftentimes know Scriptures, but to repeat one specifically
about our situation can be transformative. One of the Scriptures
that helps me when I'm feeling overwhelmed and anxious is *The
Message* version of Matthew 11:28–30. I know this Scripture in
a traditional version as the one where Jesus invites us to come
to Him when we are weary and burdened and He promises to
give us rest. Ah, the imagery in that version is helpful too. What
I need when I'm overwhelmed and weary is mostly rest. But not
necessarily a nap (although that can be helpful). What my soul

needs is to stop being overly concerned about all of the possibilities of things that can go wrong, to stop being overwhelmed by the huge, seemingly unending tasks ahead of me. I need to "get away" with God and rest, or "recover" my life.

What gives me the most peace is reading the way *The Message* describes grace—it's unforced. It's a rhythm that is at its own pace, not mine, and not anyone else's. Grace moves with me. It doesn't beat me over the head and say, "Get it done." It happens. It's free, untamed, unforced. That gives me rest. That gives me hope and relief. Ah, that's refreshing and much-needed imagery during stressful times. I thank God for grace—it's remembering that it is unforced and at a different pace that brings me much-needed rest.

Have you thought about the "unforced rhythm of grace" during your journey through the blues? How might remembering this imagery help you when you feel overwhelmed, down, or blue?

MY CONFESSION

I can have rest when I allow grace to take over. It is unforced.
Flow with grace today.

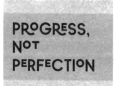

PROGRESS, NOT PERFECTION

What reminds you of the unforced rhythm of grace? Place a reminder near you so you think of the rhythm of grace often. (A picture of waves is my reminder.)

Grace-giving God: I am especially thankful for the unforced rhythm of grace. Keep me aware of the special beat of grace when I am tempted to worry or become overwhelmed. I thank you for true rest in your amazing grace. Amen.

24

A SEASON FOR IT ALL

Ecclesiastes 3:1–8

There is a time for everything, and a season for every activity under the heavens: a time to be born and a time to die, a time to plant and a time to uproot.

ECCLESIASTES 3:1–2

When struck with the blues—whether for a few days or for a longer period of time—have you ever thought that this just may be the season for recovery? Could it be the season to sit down and rest and do things just a little bit differently? After all, life does happen in seasons. Even the earth shows us that: there's fall, a time for harvesting and returning to routine; there's winter when things die and animals hibernate or sleep more; there's spring when we see new life and rebirth; and summer, when we frolic more and enjoy the longer days and many plants in full bloom.

If you're like me, you appreciate a nice long summer. You enjoy the cookouts with friends, the holidays, the family reunions, the ability to walk out of the house without a jacket or gloves or coat. I personally love my flip-flops and the slower pace of summer too. But if I'm honest, too much sun, too many "lazy" days of summer, too many outdoor cookouts can wear me out. I'm not meant to live in eternal summer. (I need to wear my fall sweaters and cute boots too!)

Likewise, as sad as it may seem, our spirits are not created to live in eternal happiness (until we get to heaven). We experience seasons of ups and downs; we hit mountaintop experiences and we utilize the valley to travel to the next experience. It doesn't even make sense to think of a mountain without considering the valley.

So, while you endure this time of being low, consider it a season. Consider it a part of the order of things. Naturally, if it lasts too long, you may need to seek more help. But if it's a part of the cycle of life, remember that Ecclesiastes proclaims that there is a time for everything. You have times to rejoice and sing, and times to mourn and lament. It's a season. And it's helpful to remember that God is with you—even in the valley (see Psalm 139:8). Sit in the season; sit in the reassurance that God sees you and hears you and is right by your side.

MY CONFESSION

In my current season, I will remember that God is right here with me.

Seasons are a natural part of life.

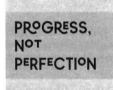

Think of some of the benefits of the natural winter season. How might these same benefits come from your emotional "winter" times?

Gracious God: Give me strength to endure this season. Help me to adjust my pace and expectations as I wait on change. Amen.

25

ACKNOWLEDGE EMOTIONS
Psalm 42:6–11

*Why, my soul, are you downcast? Why so disturbed within
me? Put your hope in God, for I will yet praise him,
my Savior and my God.*
PSALM 42:11

Our emotions are real. One way I've dealt with the blues is to acknowledge what I'm feeling. While I'm naturally an optimist (something I think helps most times), I've learned that I don't have to always rush to the positive ending. I don't need to tie a pretty bow on a package of tough stuff all the time. I do believe Romans 8:28 that all things work together for good for those who love God—but I'm also able to say that all things are not good. Some things are just awful and tough and cause me to have severe bouts of the blues.

The psalmist in today's Scripture asked the tough "why" question to his soul. He was downcast and he asked himself why. His answer comes immediately after the question and he encourages himself to put his hope in God.

When I sit with my emotions, I don't always get an answer immediately, but strangely I do usually feel better. It kind of puts things in perspective to think through why I'm downcast. It helps remind me of what may be causing dis-ease and it makes room for God's Spirit to speak to me and to help me remember where I should put my hope. I can often recall a Scripture to speak to my situation because I've acknowledged my emotions. I've sat with the discomfort and asked the why question.

It's not always easy to just pause and speak honestly about

what you are feeling or even why, and sometimes quite honestly you may not even have words for your feelings nor a reason for your blues. But, when you free yourself from having it all together and make room and take time to lament and cry out to God, as the psalmist did, you may come up with some thoughts—or you may need to release what's inside of you.

Try it today. Sit with your emotions; perhaps journal what you're feeling and what may be causing you discomfort. Ask God to speak specifically to your situation.

MY CONFESSION

I will sit with my emotions today.

You can put your hope in God for a solution to all of your problems.

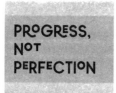

PROGRESS, NOT PERFECTION

What is causing you to feel blue and down? Ask your soul why it is downcast, and if you come up with an answer, write your answer in a journal.

All-knowing God: Give me what I need to identify the emotions causing me to feel discomfort and unease. Help me to place my hope in you for an answer. Amen.

26

NOT CRUSHED

2 Corinthians 4:7–12

*We are hard pressed on every side, but not crushed;
perplexed, but not in despair; persecuted, but not
abandoned; struck down, but not destroyed.*

2 CORINTHIANS 4:8–9

As Paul wrote to the Corinthians in today's Scripture, he presented a vivid picture with words. He acknowledged that the new Christians were having a rough time and were being attacked. They were dealing with trouble and persecution for various reasons, and he wanted to encourage them to not lose heart.

I think depression persecutes modern-day Christians; it's an attack on the mind and causes us not to see ourselves as God sees us. That causes us to forget the benefits we have through prayer and through acknowledging who God is. Who among us has not seen what God has done and can do—regardless of what we are going through? Paul's writings can remind us today not to lose heart when we are persecuted or dealing with depression.

I like to review Paul's words because they are vivid. Yes, we are hard-pressed, perplexed, and even persecuted and struck down. But after each of those descriptions, Paul acknowledges what we are *not*. We are not crushed, we are not in despair, we are not abandoned, and we are not destroyed. Paul is not saying that trouble is not present. He's not even wishing it away. But he is reminding the Corinthians and us that whatever we are going through is not the end. It's not going to take us out.

Whatever you are going through, repeat today's verses and focus especially on the words after "but not." Use these truths to keep going and keep moving as you look for brighter days. You are *not* crushed. You are *not* in despair; you are *not* abandoned. You are *not* destroyed. Hallelujah!

MY CONFESSION

Depression will not destroy me.

You may be struck down, but you are not destroyed.

Write down 2 Corinthians 4:8–9 from the version of the Bible that speaks to you most. Repeat these verses throughout the day to remind yourself that depression is not the end.

Holy God: Thank you for the reminder that this rough patch will not be the end of me. Help me to remember I'm not crushed, abandoned, or destroyed. Amen.

27

VALLEYS OF LIFE

Psalm 23

Even though I walk through the darkest valley,
I will fear no evil, for you are with me; your rod
and your staff, they comfort me.

PSALM 23:4

Valleys are talked about throughout the Bible. My favorite reference is in Psalm 23:4: "Yea, though I walk through the valley of the shadow of death . . ." (KJV—one of my Bible teachers said there's something special about quoting psalms from the King James Version).

When I'm down or blue, I also think of valleys a lot. They remind me of the low places in life. In fact, *Merriam-Webster* even uses the word *depression* in its definition. The land is lower, or depressed, in a valley.

But if we keep going with the metaphor of the valley, we also realize that valleys have a purpose and are needed. Life can't be lived on a mountain alone. And the only way to travel is in the valleys. You can't hop from mountaintop to mountaintop.

Now, I'm not here to tell you what the purpose of your valley might be. But I am here to remind you that some of life will be spent traveling in the depressed areas, the elongated periods of time that you travel along the way.

But the really good news about the valleys is in Psalm 23. Even though I'm in the valley, perhaps in the shadow of death, I don't have to be afraid. I don't have to give in to the sinking, depressing feelings. Why? Because God is with me. He promises to be with me always (Matthew 28:20). So I don't have to worry.

The valleys are not mountaintop experiences. The valleys can be pretty mundane, pretty low, not-much-to-see-here. But God is in the valleys too—and that gives me hope and a bit of encouragement to keep moving on a cloudy day in the valley.

MY CONFESSION

I may be in the valley but I'm not alone.

God walks with you through your valleys.

PROGRESS, NOT PERFECTION

Find a song or hymn that mentions the valleys. Listen to it as you walk through your valley. Two of my favorites are "The Blood Will Never Lose Its Power" by Andraé Crouch and "For Every Mountain" by Kurt Carr.

Dear God: I thank you for your promise to always be with me—even in the valleys of my life. Keep me mindful of your presence as I walk through this season. Amen.

DRWNING

Isaiah 43:1–7

*When you pass through the waters, I will be with you;
and when you pass through the rivers, they will not sweep
over you. When you walk through the fire, you will not be
burned; the flames will not set you ablaze.*

ISAIAH 43:2

If we're real honest with ourselves, we'd admit that sometimes depression, anxiety, and the blues can make us feel like we're sinking in deep water with our heads barely above the surface. I've never been close to literally drowning, but I can imagine the horror of feeling helpless as water covers your head and you can no longer hold your breath—feeling that the water is overtaking you. And sometimes that's exactly how I feel when I'm overwhelmed with life. I can't seem to grasp my breath. I can't seem to catch a break. Whether my problems are big or small, they all seem too big for me to handle. I literally feel like life is closing in on me and the waters are pushing me deeper into the unknown and unsolvable. When we're in this state, it can be tough to see past the increasing floodwaters.

It is then that the imagery outlined in Isaiah 43 becomes very, very real to me. Sometimes we read Scriptures as just words and other times we can feel them. I think it's not happenstance that God used Isaiah to share with the Israelites (and us) that life will feel insurmountable at times. It will feel like we're passing through some rough, deep, overwhelming waters. But the verse doesn't stop there—praise God. Even when life feels overwhelming like floodwaters, God makes a promise to us: He will be with us. God is right by our side in the deep, troubling waters.

When you feel overwhelmed by the waters of life, look for God, for our God has promised to be with us, no matter how we feel. Even when you feel as if you're drowning, hold on to God's promise. Look for Him even as you try to catch your breath. God is there. God is with you through the waters, through the rivers, through the fire.

MY CONFESSION

God is with me.

No matter how deep the water is, God has promised to be with you.

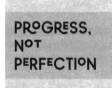

PROGRESS, NOT PERFECTION

Reflect on how you might be able to remind yourself that God is with you whether or not you feel Him. Write down ways you can keep God's promise of being with you at the forefront of your mind as you pass through troubled water. Consider reviewing ways God has been with you in the past.

God of Israel: I acknowledge that sometimes the waters of life feel like they are too much to handle, as if they will overwhelm me. But I give you thanks and praise for reminding me of your promise to be with me as I pass through the water. Amen.

A DIFFERENT FIGHT, PART I

Ephesians 6:10–17

Put on the full armor of God, so that you can take your stand against the devil's schemes. For our struggle is not against flesh and blood, but against the rulers, against the authorities, against the powers of this dark world and against the spiritual forces of evil in the heavenly realms.

EPHESIANS 6:11-12

One of my favorite exercises is a boxing workout. As I work out along with the DVD, the instructor tells me to jab and punch, cross and punch. (You do know exercise is one great tool to deal with depression—even when you don't want to, right?) While I've never been in an actual boxing ring, when I do the boxing workouts, I imagine an opponent I want to hit very hard—you know, to make the workout more effective, lol.

But seriously, picturing an opponent does help me. And to be honest, I've had a few faces of folks I worked with or even people I consider friends as my opponent in that imaginary boxing ring. But as I've grown in my Christian journey, I've replaced those human opponents' faces with what we read in Ephesians 6:11–12. It's not a person I am battling but more so the power of darkness and forces of evil. It's "principalities," according to the King James Version.

I feel that way about depression too. It can be forces of evil trying to take over our minds and spirits. It can be those imbalanced chemicals trying to make us think and do things counterintuitive to God's Spirit and what the Word of God even says about us. I declare, as I jab and cross and punch, that those forces will not take me down. Those principalities will not win. I'm in a fight—and I'm using the full armor of God to beat this. Each day, I awake, I fight, not against a person but against those forces of evil. (We'll look at the armor of God and how it helps in the next devotion.)

MY CONFESSION

I'm fighting against the evil forces that try to attack me.
You're not fighting against a person but against dark forces.

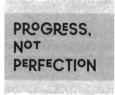

PROGRESS, NOT PERFECTION

If you are able physically, use a boxing routine; you can find one online. Do at least a small amount of exercise, and as you punch, think about knocking out the dark forces of depression.

Gracious God: I thank you for the reminder that I'm not battling against people but against forces that don't want me to win. I will rely on your strength and protection to overcome my battles. Amen.

30

A DIFFERENT FIGHT, PART 2

Ephesians 6:10–17

Stand firm then, with the belt of truth buckled around your waist, with the breastplate of righteousness in place, and with your feet fitted with the readiness that comes from the gospel of peace. In addition to all this, take up the shield of faith, with which you can extinguish all the flaming arrows of the evil one. Take the helmet of salvation and the sword of the Spirit, which is the word of God.

EPHESIANS 6:14–17

If we're going to be successful in battling the evil forces that try to knock us out, we are instructed in Ephesians to put on the full armor of God. But what is that really and how do we actually apply it to our lives so we can defeat the blues?

First, we should stand firm—securely—understanding who we are in God and just what God can do. Remember, depression can distort your mind and have you thinking you are worthless and unworthy, but when you know the truth (what God's Word says about you), you can forgo the distorted thinking and rely on the truth. Have you applied the truth of Scripture to your situation? Have you read how Jesus cast out demons and got folks right? Have you heard about how others have been healed— some with the assistance of medicine, therapy, and other mental health practices? If so, buckle these truths around your waist and hold firm to them—even on your darkest days. Believe that healing is available to you and it will come.

With the gospel of Jesus Christ fully in your mind, walk in peace. Walk, remembering who Jesus is and what He has done for you in the past, as well as what He has done for others. This transforms what you see and can help build your faith (what you don't see). Therefore, your belief becomes a shield, a protective barrier to the damages that can be done if you give in to believing the dark forces can overtake you. This shield can help you battle darkness.

Then remember to wear a helmet of salvation, a covering for your head and mind. It focuses on your gift from God, which is not only an eternal life but an abundant life (John 10:10). This abundant life may have trials, tribulations, and the blues, but it also brings joy, healing, comfort, and encouragement.

Wherever you are in your healing journey, use the whole armor of God to help you push through and battle the dark forces of the blues or depression. Yes, sometimes medicine and therapy can be used to assist the healing. Give God praise for all the tools He gives you to defeat darkness and wait with expectation that morning will come.

MY CONFESSION

I will put on the entire armor of God each day as I battle against depression.

Keep fighting, one day at a time.

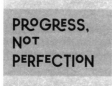

PROGRESS, NOT PERFECTION

Imagine each piece of the armor of God and how it can help you fight depression today. Throughout the day, envision yourself putting on each piece and fighting depression.

Holy God: Thank you for the tools you've given me to fight the blues. I vow to put on your full armor and keep fighting and utilize all the tools you've given me. Amen.

31

DISTORTIONS

Psalms 139:13–18

I praise you because I am fearfully and wonderfully made;
your works are wonderful, I know that full well.
PSALM 139:14

Have you ever looked at yourself in a funhouse mirror? The angles and curves in the mirror reflect light to make you appear longer, wider, thinner, larger– basically, distorted.

Depression can be a type of funhouse mirror—making your thoughts of yourself quite distorted. It whispers in your ears—or sometimes screams—that you are not worthy, that you are pitiful, that you are sick. Those voices in your head are not fair; they don't reflect the real picture of you.

God has said differently, and in blue times it's important to repeat God's words and allow them to fill your thoughts and perception of yourself.

As the psalmist says, we are created fearfully and wonderfully, meaning we have been made well, completely, beautifully. We are God's handmade creations and God knows all about us. Romans 8 reminds us that we cannot be separated from our loving God; in fact, we are more than conquerors (v. 37); that means we have the power to move mountains and defeat what is trying to distort our minds.

The distortion is not real; God's Word is. Who will you believe? Which word, or words, will you repeat to remind yourself of who you are in Christ? Surely, it's not what you are telling yourself when your spirit is distorted.

It's important when navigating the blues that you remember

who God says you are and scream those words louder than the voices in your head. You are worthy of love and care—receive it and rest in God's love.

MY CONFESSION
I am fearfully and wonderfully made.
Depression can distort who you think you are; push to remind yourself of the truth.

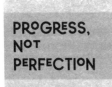

Find two or three Scripture passages that remind you of how God created you and who God designed you to be. Write these messages on note cards, on sticky notes, or in your phone to remind you of the real you.

God: I praise you for I am amazingly and wonderfully created. I know you've made me in your image and you see me as I truly am. Amen.

INTERCᴱDE
Ephesians 6:18–20

And pray in the Spirit on all occasions with all kinds of prayers and requests. With this in mind, be alert and always keep on praying for all the Lord's people.
EPHESIANS 6:18

In my quest to be made whole in mind, body, and spirit, I've read many articles and even some books on how to work through depression and the blues. Some advice is good. Some is not. Some is sensitive to the individual plight of depression; some isn't. With all of my heart, I am trying my best not to be one of those insensitive types who offer two-bit advice that will only make you feel worse. But, as a devotional writer who truly believes God's Word can be a balm and provide what we need to make it through yet another cloudy day, I offer a few tangible exercises that have helped me. These ideas are not magic pills or quick fixes but steps I have personally taken during my foggy days of depression. As I write, I pray that some of these ideas may ignite something inside of you to keep moving, keep believing, keep looking for your brighter day—one step at a time.

With that caveat, I would like to suggest intercessory prayer. It's the prayer Paul talks about in today's verse. It remembers to lift up the conditions of those around us in prayer. You see, depression has a way of making you focus on yourself. What you don't feel like doing, how low you feel, how sad you are. I know my prayer life often focused on asking God to lift up my head and part the clouds during my cloudy days. And trust me, I think those are prayers worth praying. It's an important part of this journey through the blues to take it to God in prayer. But thinking of someone else's condition and going to God on their behalf can also serve to lift your head or, more accurately, shift your focus. While calling out someone else's condition may not take away your blues, it will remind you of a few important things: (1) God is still a miracle worker and we trust God to step into our circumstances. Praying for my neighbor acknowledges that God has an answer—even when I have no clue what it is. (2) Praying for others makes me aware that there's more than my downcast soul. People around me are dealing with some serious issues—just as I am—and I want God to intervene in all of these situations.

So, while you take your concerns to God in prayer, remember to keep a list of others who need specific prayers answered too. (In my darkest days, I keep the list right near my computer and glance at it throughout the day.) Lift up the names of the people on your list. Ask God to work on their behalf—and watch what happens to your mood and your situation.

MY CONFESSION

I will lift up my brothers and sisters in need in prayer today.

When you are navigating through dark days, don't forget to intercede on behalf of others. It will shift your focus.

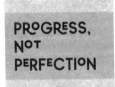

PROGRESS, NOT PERFECTION

Create a list of people you will intercede in prayer for this week. Keep the list close by so you can stop and pray for your neighbors throughout the day.

Heavenly Father: Thank you for the ability to intercede for others. While I am going through my cloudy days, I bring others to you too. I ask specifically for you to _____ for my neighbor _____. Amen.

RELEASE EXPECTATIONS
1 Samuel 17:32–40

Then Saul dressed David in his own tunic. He put a coat of armor on him and a bronze helmet on his head. David fastened on his sword over the tunic and tried walking around, because he was not used to them. "I cannot go in these," he said to Saul, "because I am not used to them." So he took them off.

1 SAMUEL 17:38-39

I believe it's important to repeat that I'm not trying to diagnose your depression; I am focusing on some things I've discovered either in myself or in others that can produce feelings that can lead to the blues. This is done in hopes that you may uncover anything that is keeping you from living your best life—the abundant life God has promised. Still, I am sharing my story, some things I've done to navigate through my depression.

I know you're probably familiar with the wonderful story of how the little shepherd boy David beat the great giant Goliath. But there's so much to this story that it's worth a revisit during days when you're trying to release yourself from the dark cloud that covers your head and makes you feel down.

When David steps up to defeat the giant no one else has defeated, Saul looks at David and imposes his own expectations on him. Saul sees David as a young boy who is not able to defeat a mighty warrior (1 Samuel 17:33). Yet, David has a strong faith based on what he has personally seen God do for him (beat off lions and bears). From there, Saul agrees to let David give this giant a try and Saul (probably with good intentions) offers David his armor. Saul wants David to use his tools to fight a giant that even Saul isn't fighting.

And I've found life can be the same way. We are living with tools and baggage that worked for some—or perhaps didn't—and we are expected to use them to fight whatever we're battling. These expectations may come from those who truly love us and they may even come from ourselves. We look up to someone who has done something we want to do—and we think we need to do it just like they did, using the same armor and tools. But one of the beauties of being created by God as unique individuals is that we operate differently. We function differently. What works for me may not work for you. Give yourself permission to release the expectations of following a certain path—even the path to healing.

Take off someone else's armor. Look for the ways God wants you to succeed. Define that success for yourself and go after it.

MY CONFESSION

I will release others' expectations of me and follow the path that is best for me.

Our unique makeup requires a unique path.

PROGRESS, NOT PERFECTION

Take time this week to think about some things you may be doing because you are expected to do them; which ones do you need to release?

Creator and Giver of life: Help me to see which path I should take. Help me to release anything that is not for me, recognizing that my path may look completely different than others', and give me the strength to be okay with that realization. Amen.

34

THOUGHT LIFE

Philippians 4:8–9

Finally, brothers and sisters, whatever is true, whatever is noble, whatever is right, whatever is pure, whatever is lovely, whatever is admirable—if anything is excellent or praiseworthy—think about such things.

PHILIPPIANS 4:8

How's your thinking? I know depression can distort what we think about ourselves and situations (see exaggeration, page 22). But it's a lifelong lesson to handle our thought life in a way that is healthy and productive. There are many Scriptures that remind us what to focus on and what not to focus on. Our minds are like the rudder of a ship . . . wherever it is pointed, it will go.

When I'm depressed, I have to be even more intentional about the things I focus on. Paul's exhortation in Philippians is always a go-to verse. Paul says that we should think about whatever is true, noble, right, pure, lovely, admirable, excellent, or praiseworthy.

It may take some work, but thinking about things, people, events that fit these descriptions can help us make it through the day—especially when we're experiencing the blues. I find that God and God's Word always fit these descriptions, and I need to think about specifics to reset my mind and get me pointed in the right direction. I try to recall something specific God has done for me that is praiseworthy; I think of something very lovely and excellent that I have seen firsthand in my life or in another's life. When the clouds come and the despair attempts to take over, I try my best to think about God's work in my life to keep going.

It takes intentionality. It takes practice. It sometimes takes more and more renewal of my thoughts—minute by minute to change the station in my mind from despair to focusing on something else.

Find a focal point today that fits the Philippians 4 "think test." Write it down and repeat it often throughout the day.

MY CONFESSION

As often as I need to, I will shift my thinking to something true, noble, right, pure, lovely, admirable, excellent, or praiseworthy.

When you are depressed, you have to be even more intentional about what you focus on.

PROGRESS, NOT PERFECTION

Write a tangible thing to think about for each description in Philippians 4:8: true, noble, right, pure, lovely, admirable, excellent, and praiseworthy.

Dear God: Give me the wisdom and strength to focus on things that are true and noble and right and pure and lovely and admirable and excellent and praiseworthy. Amen.

35

A GOOD CRY

Psalm 56:1–9

*You've kept track of my every toss and turn through
the sleepless nights, each tear entered in your ledger,
each ache written in your book.*
PSALM 56:8 MSG

One of the healthiest ways I've learned to deal with my emotions is through a good cry. Crying helps me to release some of the anguish and turmoil boiling up inside of me. While it doesn't tangibly change my situation, releasing my tears changes me. Crying reminds me that I can let some stuff go. I can release my emotions instead of allowing them to fester inside of me.

Ironically, after a good cry, I sometimes feel better. I can focus more and take a few more steps forward. Scripture provides comfort when it comes to tears too. The psalmist in Psalm 56 says that God has recorded each of his tears; He's entered them in His ledger. God knows each tear intimately. They are not lost on God; they are not in vain. God sees our pain and anguish and is keeping track of those tears.

I believe those tears won't be lost. They may be used to produce a powerful testimony that will one day help someone else. When I started talking about my depression, I received so many private messages from people who were encouraged. Why? They had suffered secretly alone for many years, and now to hear someone they knew and trusted come out and share her struggles—they felt seen. My struggle was used to help someone else. My tears and years of anguish and countless prayers weren't unnoticed and unusable.

A GOOD CRY

I don't always like to cry—but sometimes I hit the boiling point and my tears just have to flow. When my mother died, I had to make room for myself to cry. I was so used to stuffing my feelings and getting through the service and getting back to work and getting things done that I realized I hadn't given myself the time and space to truly release what I was feeling. It took sharing this with a therapist to get me to realize just how detrimental my behavior was and how I was prolonging my anguish and even preventing some healing. I needed to grieve. Releasing my tears would be a part of that healing process.

Even Jesus wept (John 11:35). Certainly we can too.

MY CONFESSION

I will let my tears flow to release emotions in a healthy way.
God collects and records each one of our tears. They are not in vain.

 **PROGRESS, NOT PERFECTION**

Find a space and place to let your tears flow. (I've known people who cry in the swimming pool or shower especially.)

God of my tears: Thank you for seeing each tear I drop. I know my tears are not in vain and I want to release my emotions. I trust you to collect them. Amen.

36

PHYSICAL EXERCISE

1 Timothy 4:7–9

For physical training is of some value, but godliness has value for all things, holding promise for both the present life and the life to come.

1 TIMOTHY 4:8

I know, when we hear this verse, we as Christians tend to focus on the fact that Paul was telling his young mentee Timothy to focus on training himself in godliness. Yes, Paul wanted Timothy to be disciplined and follow the teachings he had learned so he could live out his calling. That's pretty much what the books of 1 and 2 Timothy are about. But I think it's still important to investigate why Paul even mentioned physical training; he says it has some value. Of course, disciplining ourselves in godliness is of utmost importance, but I also think we are whole beings— and when the physical body feels good and healthy, we're better able to follow God's Spirit and discipline ourselves in godliness.

And I don't think you need to train for a marathon to reap the benefits of physical activity. Endorphins—known as happy hormones—will kick in with just some regular movement. Here are a few things I've learned on this physical exercise journey— cause I've started and stopped routines enough to have figured out some things the hard way.

- Choose activities you like. It's dancing for me, so Zumba is right up my alley.
- Choose a place and time that's good for you. If you're not a morning person, adding physical exercise at five in the morning is probably just not going to become a regular habit. Get creative. Can you walk at lunch? What about

changing into workout clothes at work so you'll be more ready to go in the afternoon? Or what are you doing in the thirty minutes between picking up the kids and running an errand for your parents? I've walked three times around the day care building before picking up my child (and it cleared my mind for my second shift of work—parenting); you know you can let them stay until six, right?! If you want to move more, you're going to have to be proactive in finding the time and place to do it.

- Do you have a friend you can go with? Walking with a friend counts as two points toward wellness—it's socializing and exercising.

- Don't give up. So, you didn't make it to your aerobics class today. Is there one tomorrow? Determine now that you will go.

I've never felt worse after a workout. It's a good investment in your physical—and mental—health.

MY CONFESSION

I will exercise because it is of value to my well-being.

Physical training is of some value. Put in a little work to receive great benefits.

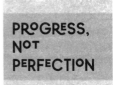

PR⚬GRESS, N⚬T PERFECTI⚬N

Plan to exercise today. Write down what you will do, at what time, and for how long. And put your plan into action.

God of all: I know physical training is of some value. I desire to move my body to make my whole being feel better. Give me the strength and discipline to move my body. Amen.

MORE ON PHYSICAL EXERCISE

3 John 2–4

*Dear friend, I pray that you may enjoy good health
and that all may go well with you, even as your soul
is getting along well.*

3 JOHN 2

Because exercise is so vital to not only your physical well-being but your mental well-being, I'm adding another reflection on what I've learned—particularly on days I don't want to exercise.

You don't have to want to do it to be able to do it. I often have to trick myself to exercise. I tell myself only twenty minutes, a quick walk around the block (getting outside is a treat for me most times). Or, I turn on some music and pretend I'm that world-class dancer in my head. And all of our modern-day technology has made it easier than ever to find just the right workout for you; try typing what you're looking for in your favorite search engine: ten-minute walk, upper-body workout for beginners, dance party with '80s music. Trust me, there's something there just for you, my friend.

My cousin once told me to try to exercise at the same time each day. It's a signal to your brain that it's time—and you won't keep putting it off if you have a scheduled time.

I've also read that envisioning yourself exercising can help too. Picture yourself sprinting, dancing, riding a bike to prepare your mind to get ready to move your body.

Give yourself a nonfood treat when you have successfully

completed an exercise goal. Watch your favorite TV show (either while on the exercise bike or as your reward for getting in twenty minutes) or read the article you've had bookmarked. Consider calling a friend to chat with while walking around the block (you can use an earpiece but be cautious of your environment too). And it goes without saying, your playlist is very important. Throw in some fast-paced oldies that remind you of the days you really enjoyed music. Even getting to listen to my favorite audiobook has gotten me to lace up my gym shoes and walk when I didn't really want to.

MY CONFESSION

I will care for my physical body through exercise—even when I don't want to.

Focus on your well-being over how you feel when it comes to getting in some exercise.

Think of an after-exercise reward you would enjoy, then get moving.

Holy God: Give me what I need to take the steps to exercise my physical body. I know it is connected to my mental well-being and I desire to live a full life in good health. Amen.

38

FIGHTING TEMPTATION

1 Corinthians 10:11–13

No temptation has overtaken you except what is common to mankind. And God is faithful; he will not let you be tempted beyond what you can bear. But when you are tempted, he will also provide a way out so that you can endure it.

1 CORINTHIANS 10:13

The night before my grandmother died, she did what she did every other Saturday night. She laid out her clothes for church in the morning. When my grandfather—along with my mother and her sister—returned to my grandmother's house after having been at the hospital where she was pronounced dead, they found her nylons, dress, and undergarments stretched out on her couch. We talked about this display of her determination for many years. You see, that's just what Mama Olivia did the night before she was attending church. Because her mind was focused and determined to be up and ready for her early morning church service, the night before she always laid out what she was going to wear.

I love this memory of my grandmother. It's a great reminder of how getting ready, preparing even before the next day, can put us in the mindset we need for that day. Another friend usually lays out her workout clothes the night before when she goes to bed—down to the socks tucked away in her gym shoes. It helps her get in that early morning workout. She doesn't even have to think about finding her socks. She's set and ready to go.

Sometimes when we're facing the blues, we need to adopt the attitude of my grandmother and my dear friend. We need to do the things we need to do to position ourselves closer to our goals. It won't be easy to get up and get out the door, but knowing what we're putting on takes away yet another decision that needs to be made when we already don't want to go. Preparing food ahead of time can help us eat better when we're actually hungry (cause if you've ever tried making a decision to eat well when you're hungry, you know it's a lot harder; temptation is lurking and will get you). Agreeing to ride with a friend—or better yet to pick up someone—for a social event will make it more likely that we make it, although isolation is setting up her temptress tricks to get us to stay home. Sometimes you've just got to trick the body so the mind will follow. It's for your good—one more step toward being okay—whether you feel it or not.

MY CONFESSION

I will fight temptation by being prepared even if I need to trick myself to do some things.

Sometimes you have to trick yourself to get you closer to your goal.

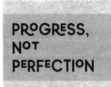

PROGRESS, NOT PERFECTION

What would you like to do today that's good for you? How might you employ special strategies to get it done?

Holy One: Thank you for the reminder that you always have a way out for me when I am tempted. I know there are ways I can endure. Amen.

39

CHOOSE GENTLE
Galatians 5:22–25

But the fruit of the Spirit is love, joy, peace, forbearance, kindness, goodness, faithfulness, gentleness and self-control. Against such things there is no law.

GALATIANS 5:22-23

During one of those rare times I decided to be vulnerable and let a friend know I was struggling, I was feeling out of it and overwhelmed. She said some words that still stick with me today. "Be gentle with yourself." (Thank God for friends who have a timely word!)

She gave me permission to actually do what the Word says: be gentle. Gentleness is a by-product of walking in God's Spirit. It comes when I lean on God's Spirit. It makes me season my words—and actions—with love and care.

And that same gentleness I use with others needs to be turned around and used on myself—especially when I'm not feeling my best. I need special care when I'm down and struggling, but often I beat myself up and try to force myself to "get it together." But why can't I treat myself better when I need it? I do it when I have a cold. I feel free to take a nap, I pick up the water bottle more intentionally, and I treat myself to hot soup and tea—in an effort to care for my body while it fights a virus.

Treat yourself gently when you're not feeling your best emotionally. Naturally, you may need to seek additional help if this feeling continues for more than a few weeks or interferes with you getting things done continually. But some days, give a gentle nod to yourself to take it easy, to rest, to speak words of love and gentleness to yourself instead of trying to force yourself to do some things. Treat yourself like you'd treat a loved one—after all, you are loved.

MY CONFESSION

I will be gentle with myself today.

If you can give yourself grace when you have a cold, you can also accept grace when you're not emotionally well.

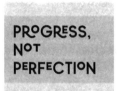

PROGRESS, NOT PERFECTION

Create a list of things you can do to be gentle with yourself. Now, do some of those things and care for your spirit.

Loving God: Show me how to be gentle with myself and to care for my spirit. Help me to love myself as I love others, remembering your unconditional love throughout this day. Thank you. Amen.

40

WHEN YOU FEEL BETTER, DO BETTER . . .

James 1:4–6

If any of you lacks wisdom, you should ask God,
who gives generously to all without finding fault,
and it will be given to you.

JAMES 1:5

This mantra got me through many days of the blues: When you feel better, do better . . . And when you don't, take the pressure off of yourself and sit down.

You know there are just some seasons in this life when you can do more. You have the energy and the will to organize those closets. You might decide to take up a hobby and can actually stick with it. You want to get out; you want to try a new recipe; shoot, you just might want to date and post your profile on a dating site (if you're single).

But then there are times when just thinking of any of those tasks can send you into a tailspin. When I was in the middle of my depression state—the foggy, numb kind—getting out of bed to catch the number four bus to head downtown (only a few miles from my house) was a major chore. If I got to work, I considered this day a success. If I turned in my work on time, proclaim it a gold-star day. Thankfully, I worked in an environment with flexible deadlines. And quite frankly, my past work had proven I did make deadlines and I did do my work well, so my bosses were generally less worried about my ability to deliver. This is where overachiever syndrome pays off; people know your ability, and if you just do minimal work, you can "fake" it for a minute and still look like you're achieving something.

Of course, the high-achiever syndrome does have a downside; you have to lower your own personal standards for yourself . . . and that can be hard and troubling and our biggest hurdle. Looking back, I know my work wasn't always my best during these years; perhaps I didn't think of many new ideas and just completed the necessary tasks. But you know what? That was okay for that stage of my life.

When you don't feel well, lower your standards. Figure out what must be done and do it. The other stuff (like the closet) will be there when you feel better. And trust me, organizing a closet won't feel so painful when you're healthier (right now, I actually enjoy reading and trying to implement the helpful home-organization tips I can find online).

Take a moment to go easy on yourself—it could help you get better sooner.

MY CONFESSION

I will go easy on myself today.

Lower your standards—just until you feel better.

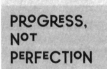

PROGRESS, NOT PERFECTION

Practice going easy on yourself. Look for a task or circumstance where you can purposefully lower your standards and do it.

My Lord: I know you know all about me. Show me what has to be done today and what I can let go. Help me to release guilt and shame and care for myself. Amen.

NO SHAME

Romans 8:1–4

Therefore, there is now no condemnation for those who are in Christ Jesus, because through Christ Jesus the law of the Spirit who gives life has set you free from the law of sin and death.
ROMANS 8:1-2

Did you know that May 5 is National Silence the Shame Day? There seems to be a day for everything, but I can get behind this one. It's designed to increase awareness around the need for mental health wellness—everything from affordable and accessible health care for mental health challenges to education to recovery tools. But it's interesting the folks who started the day chose the slogan "silence the shame."

There's a lot of shame around mental health issues. I'm not sure why. We tend to think less of our mental health and those who struggle with maintaining it (probably everyone in some form or another). For some reason, we see care for the mental state differently than for other parts of the body. But it's not. It's all really tied together. When your body is sick, your mental state usually suffers. Hey, I've been in a hospital bed for a physical ailment and felt really, really sad and hopeless. Just being released and getting to sleep in my own bed made a big difference. And postpartum depression is real and related to the hormones in the body after delivering a child. Some people struggle with hormonal imbalances at different phases of their lives—like women in menopause. Some medications have depression as a side effect and people have been known to be more depressed after surgeries. Yet, so many of us struggle in shame and in silence when we are depressed, experience anxiety and panic attacks, or have the blues.

But the Bible has a word about shame. We should let it go and walk in the freedom of knowing Christ. He has released us from shame, and whenever it creeps up again, we need to recall what God has done and walk in that reality.

I think they are right on May 5: we need to silence shame. But we need to go further and expel it from our lives. There's no shame in this game. Our mental well-being should be a priority in our lives and in the lives of all human beings. We didn't cause this pain and we don't need to suffer in shame and silence. The more we speak out, the bolder we get about seeking help and balance, the sooner May 5 is no longer just a day with a catchy slogan.

MY CONFESSION

I will not be ashamed when I suffer with mental illness.

National Silence the Shame Day is designed to increase awareness around the need for mental health wellness.

PROGRESS, NOT PERFECTION

What will you do today to silence the shame?

Almighty: I know there's no condemnation or shame in you; I'm thankful for how you've released me from sin and shame through Christ. Help me to release any shame I have around mental illness as I seek to become whole. Amen.

A LITTLE LIGHT
John 8:12–18

When Jesus spoke again to the people, he said, "I am the light of the world. Whoever follows me will never walk in darkness, but will have the light of life."
JOHN 8:12

One of the most thoughtful gestures a friend did for me in the midst of one of my struggles with depression was to give me a light box. She was one friend I had shared my struggles with and she too experienced periods of sadness especially during our dark, gray winters in Chicago. My friend found light boxes and purchased one for each of us.

While I'm not here to prescribe any specific treatment, I can share how my light box worked for me in addition to many other therapies that supported my overall well-being. I sat the light on my desk and turned it on for a short period of time each day. As I worked, the light illuminated my space in a way designed to expose me to more brightness. It is believed that light therapy will lift most people's mood if used consistently for a period of time.

As I think about how light therapy works, I can't help but think about Jesus's description of himself as the light of the world and perhaps why He chose that metaphor. Is it because light draws out darkness? Is it because light illuminates a path? Is it because light lifts the spirit when it is steeped in darkness?

In an effort to be practical and still spiritual-minded in my treatment of depression, I think of Jesus as the light of the world every time I use my light box. I sometimes use it to maintain well-being because I know what is approaching in the upcoming season and I want to get ahead of the game. Reflecting on who Jesus is can give a similar lift. He's the beacon; He's a mood lifter; He's illumination in darkness.

As I consider light therapy, I will also recall the Light of the world and what He means to me.

MY CONFESSION

I will seek light spiritually and physically today.

Light therapy seeks to draw us closer to light in dark days.

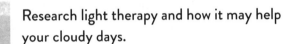

PROGRESS, NOT PERFECTION

Research light therapy and how it may help your cloudy days.

Light of the world: Thank you for illuminating my path. When my days feel extra dark, remind me of what your light stands for and why you are the light of the world. Amen.

43

ADVENTUROUS LIFE?

Romans 8:14–17

This resurrection life you received from God is not a timid, grave-tending life. It's adventurously expectant, greeting God with a childlike "What's next, Papa?" God's Spirit touches our spirits and confirms who we really are. We know who he is, and we know who we are: Father and children. And we know we are going to get what's coming to us—an unbelievable inheritance! We go through exactly what Christ goes through. If we go through the hard times with him, then we're certainly going to go through the good times with him!
ROMANS 8:15–17 MSG

I can be one of the first to admit that life can seem awfully routine. Wake up, pray (hopefully), get a cup of coffee, get dressed, go to school, go to work, come home, eat dinner, sleep, rinse and repeat. Every day (well, except on weekends if you have that type of schedule). For me, the routine of life and boredom produced some dark days, days it felt hard to get up and function. After a prolonged period of time, this led to more severe depression.

But understanding life as an adventure with God has helped when I'm in a rut or thinking of life as routine and mundane. I love the way *The Message* version of the Bible describes our relationship with God in one of my all-time favorite chapters of the Bible: Romans 8. (Try reading it all; it can be heavy reading, but it's filled with some amazingly awesome descriptions of just what Christ has done for us.)

The Message describes our resurrection life—the life we have after believing in Christ—as an adventure. We're not sitting around waiting to be beamed up to heaven or wondering when we will die and live with Christ forever. No, it's an expectant life where we relate to God as a child would. We ask, "What's next?" knowing that God is with us and leading us into adventures.

While these adventures may not be actual roller-coaster rides at an amusement park, *The Message* version sure does make it seem like this resurrection life is going to be something fun and exciting. And you know what? When we view life as a journey with God, we can treat it like an adventure. We will encounter trouble and issues, but we also use our faith to look for the message God is sending even in the spiral of life. We recognize that we're not on this ride of life alone. We're sitting right next to our Papa—and He's sitting next to us, riding with us through the good and through the bad.

So, if you feel you're in a routine pattern of boredom today, think of this day as a day to ride a roller coaster with God. What's next? What will you learn? What will you see and experience? It just may be enough to get you excited about the adventure of life again.

MY CONFESSION

I will think of today as an adventure with God, looking to see what is next and knowing that He is right by my side.

Life is an adventure filled with ups and downs.

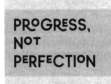

PROGRESS, NOT PERFECTION

Walk throughout this day as if you're on a roller coaster with God. What do you see? What do you experience? How do you feel? Let God know.

Merciful Father: Lead me and guide me on this journey of life. I'm so grateful that you are right by my side and will help me with whatever I encounter this day. Amen.

44

OUR WITNESSES

Hebrews 12:1–11

Therefore, since we are surrounded by such a great cloud of witnesses, let us throw off everything that hinders and the sin that so easily entangles. And let us run with perseverance the race marked out for us, fixing our eyes on Jesus, the pioneer and perfecter of faith. For the joy set before him he endured the cross, scorning its shame, and sat down at the right hand of the throne of God.
HEBREWS 12:1-2

Sometimes when I'm in a worship service at my home church, I take a look around at the congregation praising God, and I smile. Sometimes I purposefully study the people raising their hands, shouting, or even sitting silently with a reverent look on their faces. I think about those I know and some of the prayer requests and testimonies they have shared with me or our entire congregation.

I think of the woman we prayed for when her son was born with abnormalities. I see the man who lost his wife in a tragedy. I look at the one who endured several rounds of chemo and I even look at the one who admitted to dealing with depression—and I join them in praise to God.

Witnessing these people worshipping God is a reminder that they are overcomers. Life has not been easy for them, or to borrow from Langston Hughes, it hasn't been a "crystal stair," and I know just a bit of their stories. But seeing them rejoice and give God praise is a reminder that I too can overcome. God doesn't have any favorites. What God has done for these people, I know God can do for me.

I think of the struggles of my own family and ancestors. Life was not a bed of roses. It was tough, filled with both internal and external challenges. Yet, I'm here, birthed from two imperfect people who had their own set of challenges.

I don't know how my story will turn out, how my illnesses will heal, but I can look around and find hope in the stories of others. Surely there's hope in the stories of others. We can overcome through their testimonies. We can find the needed encouragement to pursue healing by recalling their triumphant stories.

If you haven't read Hebrews 11 in a while, consider reading it and thinking about each obstacle those listed in the hall of faith overcame. How can their stories inspire you to keep moving and hoping in Christ?

MY CONFESSION

When I look at my cloud of witnesses, I realize that I too can overcome.

Many have overcome with the help of God.

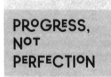

PROGRESS, NOT PERFECTION

Interview a person who has struggled with depression. Ask them what has helped them overcome and keep going.

God of my ancestors: Remind me of all you have done in the past to help others overcome. Help me to find strength in their stories and testimonies as I determine to keep moving forward. Amen.

LIFTED EYES

Psalm 121

I lift up my eyes to the mountains—where does my help come from? My help comes from the LORD, the Maker of heaven and earth.

PSALM 121:1-2

Where's your focus? Depression can cause you to think only of your problems. It can make you think there's no hope and things will not get better—things will remain the same and you will always feel like you feel currently.

But, when you're able to shift your focus beyond your current condition and feelings, you may be able to see more. Today's verses remind us to look up for help. While it is tempting to look inward and focus on our emotions and feelings (this has its place), it's just as important to look outward and upward, casting our gaze on who God is and what God is capable of.

Casting your gaze on God's creation can serve as a reminder of who God is . . . and don't we need that reminder on cloudy days? For one period of my life, I woke up to the recording of Hezekiah Walker and the lines of the song "Jesus Is My Help." Those words rang through my home each morning and guided my day. I didn't always feel like Jesus was my help—because I often awoke to the numb feeling of not wanting to get out of bed. But hearing those words reminded me to shift my focus. To look to God for help—help to get out of bed, help to do what needed to be done on this day, and help to keep moving forward.

Jesus is our help. Lift your focus to Him and look for ways He sends you help.

MY CONFESSION

Jesus is my help. I will lift my focus and look for the help God sends.

Your help is present. Look for it.

....

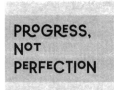
PROGRESS, NOT PERFECTION

Listen to Hezekiah Walker's "Jesus Is My Help" and walk into this day expecting God to help you.

....

Lord: I lift my eyes toward the heavens, knowing that you are my help. Give me what I need to see all of the ways you provide help to me this day. Amen.

GETTING WELL, PART I

John 5:1–9

Here a great number of disabled people used to lie—the blind, the lame, the paralyzed. One who was there had been an invalid for thirty-eight years. When Jesus saw him lying there and learned that he had been in this condition for a long time, he asked him, "Do you want to get well?"
JOHN 5:3-6

The message of the man at the pool has both blessed and haunted me—in different segments of my journey. First of all, Jesus's question to the man who was an invalid is startling. Jesus asks the man who apparently cannot move if he wants to be well. We don't know the man's exact condition, but it is clear from the text that he needed someone to help him into the healing pool; he couldn't just get in the pool by himself, so he thought. Why would Jesus start off by asking the man if he wanted to be well? This poor man had been unable to move for at least thirty-eight years—that's a lifetime. That's years and years of sitting and watching others walk; that's years and years of watching others live a life he probably desired. This man was sitting on the sidelines as the game of life continued—only he was not let into the game; he sat and watched paralyzed as the rest of the world seemed to go right along with their lives.

Isn't that how depression feels? You're living in your body, feeling stuck and sometimes paralyzed, while the world is going on with business as usual. The people surrounding you look and act normal, living their lives and enjoying activities.

I sometimes see the question Jesus asked this man as insensitive, which also causes me to think about the questions others ask of those suffering with depression or any other form of mental impairment. But at the same time, I read Jesus's question and consider its significance. Sometimes being stuck and paralyzed for so long can make us think there's no other way: *This is it. I won't ever get my turn in the pool. I'm stuck here. This is my life. I'll do the best I can to manage this condition as I watch others live their lives.*

But Jesus, who cares enough to stop and notice this invalid, poses the all-important question. He wants to know if the man wants to get well. Other translations say Jesus asked if the man wanted to be made whole, become healthy, or be healed.

Adopting the compassion and care Jesus must have carried with Him, I want you to ask yourself that question too. There's no judgment. I know how it feels to be stuck. I know it's not as easy or simple as "snapping out of it." But I do know some steps have to be taken to begin to heal, and often the first one is envisioning something different, moving, pushing, and getting the help we need. So, as we begin to look at healing, ask yourself, What does it mean to be whole? What does it look like for you to be whole and healthy? Begin with the vision.

MY CONFESSION

I do want to be whole and healed.

With compassion and care, Jesus looked on the man and asked if he wanted to be made whole. With the same compassion and care, ask yourself the same question. Amen.

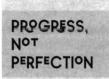

PROGRESS, NOT PERFECTION

Journal about what it would mean for you to be whole and healthy. What does this look like for you? What would you be able to do?

Compassionate Lord: I want to be made whole. Show me the steps I need to take toward healing. In your name. Amen.

47

GETTING WELL, PART 2
John 5:1–9

"Sir," the invalid replied, "I have no one to help me into the pool when the water is stirred. While I am trying to get in, someone else goes down ahead of me." Then Jesus said to him, "Get up! Pick up your mat and walk." At once the man was cured; he picked up his mat and walked.
JOHN 5:7–9

As you envision healing and wholeness—how you define getting well—let's continue to journey with the man who had been paralyzed or stuck in his same position for thirty-eight years. His healing appears to have come suddenly when Jesus inquired about his desire to be healed. Insensitive pastors have screamed from pulpits that all the man had to do was pick up his mat and walk; even more insensitive loved ones may have screamed these words at you too as many just don't understand depression and its paralyzing impact on its targets. "Just get up"; "Just snap out of it"; "Just get up and put on some clothes." (Yes, I've heard that one—as if getting dressed would fix all that ails me!)

But something I have taken from these sermons on the man at the pool is that he was definitely stuck and he had rehearsed his excuses for not being able to get into the pool. Again, I'm not judging him; I get it. He had tried to get to the pool, but apparently every time he had mustered up all the effort he could, someone else got ahead of him. I imagine he had stopped trying because he was defeated. He couldn't get to the pool before anyone else.

Seeking our wholeness can feel awfully defeating. I can rattle off the excuses I had: It's hard. I have too much to do so I can't go to therapy. How will I pay for a therapist? How will I even find a good one? I can't exercise because I can barely get out of bed. I don't feel like cooking healthy foods to care for myself better. I don't want to go to another doctor. (Now, feel free to insert the ones you've used as the reason you cannot be healed.)

But, something was different this time for the man. He was speaking to Jesus and Jesus was speaking to him about his condition. This doesn't mean it wasn't still hard for him to get up; it doesn't mean he wasn't still paralyzed with fear or defeated by yesterday's attempt. It means he was talking to someone who could do something about his condition—if the man was willing to get up, to take the first step.

Speaking to Jesus about our excuses—being specific, open, and honest—can lead to solutions, supernatural strength, and healing. Are you willing to take the first step and keep pressing toward healing?

MY CONFESSION

I want to bring my excuses to Jesus today.

Speak to Jesus about your condition and allow Him to speak to you about your condition.

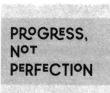

PROGRESS, NOT PERFECTION

List all of the reasons you've made for not seeking healing and wholeness. Be honest and open and share your reasons with the Lord in prayer. Be open to hearing ways around your hurdles.

Dear God: Speak to me about my condition. I want to be made whole; show me how. Tell me where to turn and who to seek for help. Strengthen me when I am weary and feel defeated. I do want to be well. Amen.

48

WRITE THE VISION (GETTING WELL, PART 3)

Habakkuk 2:2–3

Then the LORD replied: "Write down the
revelation and make it plain on tablets so
that a herald may run with it."
HABAKKUK 2:2

As we look at being made whole, I believe it's important to understand what we want—what wholeness looks like for you personally. Jesus asked the invalid if he wanted to be made whole and the man answered with his reasons he could not get into the pool. That was not the question. Perhaps if the man had written out his vision, he would have better been able to answer Jesus. If he had been focused on what he truly wanted and not what held him back, he might have answered with a resounding yes. Thankfully, Jesus had a plan for the man anyway and went ahead and healed him.

What can we do to better understand what wholeness looks like? Sometimes when you're so down and have been for a long time like the invalid, you can forget what wholeness looks like. You may not really know what it feels like to be well in your body and mind and soul.

When God gave the prophet Habakkuk a vision about His beloved Israel, God instructed the prophet to go ahead and write down what God had revealed. Not only was he to write down a word picture of restoration for God's people, but Habakkuk also needed to make it plain. Why? So even a runner—someone moving quickly and on the go—could read what was written. Even a messenger who had to run would know what the vision was. That's pretty clear. That's pretty certain. That's amazing.

How clear is your goal? What do you really want? What will make you whole and how will you respond? I prayed the prayer, "God, make me whole," for many years. I even read Stormie Omartian's book with the same title. I still remember taking the bus to work and a man seeing the title and commenting that that was his prayer too. For me, I had to dig deep into my memory and think about times I felt healthy and whole. Physically, I could see pictures where my smile was bright and my eyes even smiled. My skin color was bronze-like and glowing, my hair shining, and I felt happy. I'm sure I had issues or problems, but they didn't show up on my face. I had somehow turned them over to God and was walking in peace and looking forward to what was to come.

That's a part of my vision of living whole. I've had days when I was there and years when I wasn't. But when I write down how wholeness feels to me, I can focus more on the goal. I can reach for fruit instead of candy (because I know that makes me feel better); I can even push myself to exercise and join my prayer call (because I know what a good workout and a powerful prayer can do!).

MY CONFESSION

I will write down what it feels like to be whole.

Write the vision and make it plain. Know what you want and what you're working toward.

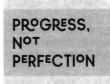

PROGRESS, NOT PERFECTION

Look for a picture of yourself during a time when you felt whole—or at least better than you do now. Use it to write down what it means for you to feel whole and create a vision for your wholeness.

God: I desire to be made whole. I want to be well in my mind, body, and soul. Help me to capture what this looks like for me in a written vision so that it can be plain and clear what I'm looking for. Amen.

AN ABUNDANT LIFE

John 10:1–10

The thief comes only to steal and kill and destroy; I have come that they may have life, and have it to the full.
JOHN 10:10

One of my favorite verses is John 10:10, where Jesus proclaims to His followers why He has come to earth. After setting up an analogy of a gatekeeper and sheep, saying that sheep listen to the voice of their shepherd, the gatekeeper, Jesus, reminds us that the enemy's purpose is to steal and kill and destroy. However, the antithesis of our enemy, Jesus, has come to give us not only an eternal life—but an abundant, full life.

Let's unpack what that abundant life looks like and how envisioning it can help us even on cloudy days. For me, abundant means I have what I need—and this goes much further than financially. In an abundant life, I am whole, I am joyous, I am worry free, I am complete and healthy. Anything that hinders me from living in that space can be considered a thief, someone who is here to steal from me or destroy me. I can't give in to a thief. I can't sit by and let a thief come into my home and not try to get back what belongs to me. So, when I feel myself sinking into anything less than what I feel is my best life—or abundant life—I recall Jesus's words. Sometimes I need to read John 10:10 over and over again to remind myself of what Jesus wants for me. This makes me get up and shift things around so I can experience wholeness and completeness.

Living wholly and abundantly does take work on my part. I need to be vigilant and look out for joy stealers and put them in their place as I journey toward wholeness and experience completeness in my mind, body, and spirit. It's a journey—but it's well worth it. I push to do what I need to do to live the life Jesus has promised me.

MY CONFESSION

I will live an abundant life.

Jesus came to give you a full, abundant, and complete life.

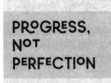

PROGRESS, NOT PERFECTION

Write about *how* an abundant life looks to you. What is attempting to steal or kill that life? How can you be vigilant and overcome the thief? What steps will you take today to stop the enemy from taking away your abundant life?

Lord of all: Thank you for the promise of abundant life. I receive it and will do all I can to live fully and completely as you have promised. Amen.

PTSD

John 11:32–37

Jesus wept.
JOHN 11:35

Allow me to insert a Black pop culture reference here. I dare say every Black person of a certain age reading this will know what I mean when I say grief or your response to trauma can sneak up on you like it did Florida Evans when she dropped that punch bowl and said the three words on the infamous episode of '70s TV sitcom *Good Times*. Yep, you know the scene. For my non-Black readers or those who just may not recall that: google Florida Evans and punch bowl.

Florida broke that bowl after her husband's funeral. She had been running around taking care of her family, thanking all who dropped off casseroles, and basically saying she was "fine." But at some point, her dam literally broke and she had to release her tears and begin her real grieving process.

I get Florida's response—for several reasons. During times of grief, it can be tough; you have services to plan, things to figure out, and so on. (See page 40 for the story of the time I said I couldn't cry after my mom died.) But delaying the flow of tears—or however you express your grief and emotions—only creates a mounting set of emotions that will explode, sometimes at the worst times.

When we don't deal with our emotions adequately—and even sometimes when we do—we sustain what was once most commonly associated with servicemen and servicewomen returning from war—post-traumatic stress disorder. Now, we've realized that this disorder can impact anyone who has endured trauma, which can include violence, abuse, or any type of loss. Basically, whenever you have experienced a battle—something you've had to endure—PTSD can creep up on you.

I find sometimes we don't even realize we've been through trauma. We've been so focused on holding it together like Florida Evans that we don't realize our bodies' and minds' response. We've been in a special mode—regardless of how well we think we've been doing—and we need to treat the trauma. We need to care for ourselves in a special way, which often can involve therapy, medicine, and tools that help us when we are triggered.

It's important to acknowledge what we've been through. Yes, we can rejoice and thank God for helping us overcome—and we should. But we must also remember to reflect and treat our minds and bodies for the trauma. When Jesus observed the grief of Lazarus's loved ones—and perhaps when He realized His good friend was dead even if for a moment—Jesus wept. He shed tears for His friend and the hurt others were enduring. Releasing our emotions is a natural and healthy way to deal with loss.

MY CONFESSION

I will release my emotions.

In order to heal from trauma, you need to face what you've been through.

PROGRESS, NOT PERFECTION

Create time and space to reflect on trauma you've endured. How might you release emotions that can be stored up from these incidents? Who or what might you turn to for help?

Lord: Show me what I need to acknowledge and release to you. I desire to move past traumatic incidents and continue to trust you. I know you are a healer and I believe in your power to heal me. Amen.

MORE PTSD

1 Peter 5:6–11

Cast all your anxiety on him because he cares for you.
1 PETER 5:7

Think about how our world changed in 2020. Many of us who were not essential workers were sent home for two weeks to work remotely (if we were "lucky"). Children were told to take two weeks of schoolwork home. For my child, that two weeks turned into eighteen months before she entered the school building again and saw her friends. We were told varying information about a disease and how it spread; we went to stores and hoarded toilet tissue as if it were the end of the world. We scrambled for groceries and prayed we had enough money to purchase food for an uncertain period of time. Still others went out to continue working, now wearing masks and wondering about an unknown pathogen.

To get through the pandemic, I feel like I held my breath and prayed. *Lord, keep us safe.* So what happened when it was time to exhale (whenever that may have been, seeing that the virus is still circulating with all its variants)? The summer after vaccinations were widely available, I knew I needed some extra help. I needed to cry. I needed to release. I needed to hug my father and sister and other loved ones I didn't get to see for two years.

When we've endured trauma of any kind, it's important to pay attention to our mental health. We need to exhale. Let it out. If possible, plan a day (or ideally more days) with nothing to do but care for your soul. A long walk, a hot bath, a cup of a warm beverage with a friend or alone—do this and do it again and again. Trauma isn't developed in one day; it's the sustained position of dealing with a tough situation. We've all lived through a pandemic. That's trauma regardless of what advantages you may have experienced. People died all around us. Politicians bickered. Science morphed; new discoveries occurred often and we were left wondering what to believe.

Oh, we need to collectively exhale and breathe. I don't know where we are on the pandemic trajectory when you're reading this (but, Lord, I hope it's over), but if life has taught me anything, something else may have occurred to put you in trauma. Exhale and don't discount the strength you mustered up and the impact that living under such stress and anxiety for an extended period of time has had on you.

Wherever you are right now, give yourself permission to exhale and to reflect on how you made it, and give your soul time to heal. This season may be your season to exhale . . . and to allow the pieces of your soul to slowly mend back together to produce a healthier, sturdier you!

MY CONFESSION

I will give myself time and special care to heal after trauma, and even in the midst of trauma.

We all need to exhale and breathe.

PROGRESS, NOT PERFECTION	Plan a time to care for yourself especially after trauma. What will you do? How will you incorporate your caring activity into your life?

NAVIGATING THE BLUES

*God of my weary years: You know what I've been
through. Only you know the ins and the outs, the
heaviness of my soul. Help me to lay down my cares at
your feet as I heal and mend. Amen.*

52

BREATH WORK
Genesis 2:6–8

*Then the L*ORD *God formed a man from the dust of the
ground and breathed into his nostrils the breath of life, and
the man became a living being.*
GENESIS 2:7

During one of my dry seasons—you know, the ones where you
feel disconnected from God—I tried focusing on my breath. With
some practice and intentionality, focusing on God as I breathed
in and breathed out reminded me of my source and strength. Reflecting on God while taking in air reminded me that I am only
alive because of God's provisions. I cannot do anything without
the breath of life, which is given by God as Genesis reminds us.
We would be dust—or nothing—had God not breathed into the
first human's nostrils and given the man life.

So when I'm having trouble getting my day started or getting
past a roadblock—either because of the blues, stress, or other
reasons—I try to remember to be intentional about breath work.
I take what I call "breath walks" hourly until I feel better. On
these walks, I find a path (normally the hallway in my home)
to walk up and down three times. As I inhale, I thank God for
breath. As I exhale, I thank God for breath. Throughout the
walk, I take deep breaths in and release long breaths out. Simply
breathing and thinking of God gives me a renewed mind and the
walking renews my body. And completing three treks up and
down (regardless of how short or long they are) also gives me
a sense of accomplishment—something I need on rough days. I
try to alleviate distractions (like refusing to pick up a sock in the

hallway or straighten a crooked picture as I pass by) and I look forward to the next walk—and I clear my mind and connect to God.

At one point I chided myself for not being connected to God—who gives me life. Shouldn't breathing remind me of God? I now try not to chide myself but to pick up the practice and inhale and exhale with my great God on my mind. Try it. You can even take in and release the big breaths from your seat if you cannot get up and walk. Just be intentional as you breathe in and out and thank God for the breath of life.

MY CONFESSION

I know God has given me each breath I take. I will thank Him for each one.

God's breath has given me life.

....

PROGRESS, NOT PERFECTION

Plan to take breath walks each hour today.

....

God of life: Thank you for my every breath. Help me to praise you as I inhale and exhale this day. Renew my strength with each breath I take. Amen.

53

RESTING

Mark 4:35–41

Jesus was in the stern, sleeping on a cushion. The disciples woke him and said to him, "Teacher, don't you care if we drown?"

MARK 4:38

To me, one of the great things about the invention of social media is the popularity of funny memes. These pictures with quick sayings often tickle me and stay in my mind—the power of images and words. One particular meme that has been circulating is of a man sleeping with the caption: "Jesus took naps. Be like Jesus."

Amen to that! If I were to create a meme for this book, I'd build on that one. I'd share with anyone dealing with the blues the importance of rest. For some reason—that's probably cultural— we think we have to do everything. We think our hands have to be on it to make it right. We think the house will fall apart if we stop. As caretakers of the world—caring for parents, children, others—we have given in to the notion that we are needed, and if we stop to rest or pause, life will not continue.

Can we just look at Jesus's example to totally refute that claim? In today's Scripture Jesus had been busy. The pace of Mark's entire gospel makes it seem like Jesus was on the go. He had been teaching and healing and performing miracles, but even He knew He could use a good rest. He took His inner circle and pulled away from the crowd. And He rested; He slept on a cushion on the boat. Apparently, He wasn't driving the boat; He wasn't pointing to let everyone know which direction to go; He wasn't teaching or preparing a meal. Jesus was doing some good sleeping, caring for His mind, body, and soul through restorative sleep.

I'm usually amazed when I stop and think about how little we rest as a culture (Western and otherwise). Even on days off, we're usually running errands or cleaning or tackling that pile of laundry. I'm not saying take all those days off—but ask yourself, What would happen if you rested? What would happen if during your cloudy days, you took more time off to sleep? Or would you have as many cloudy days if you built true self-care and rest into your schedule? I know I wouldn't. Burnout is one of the causes I've identified that contribute to my depression. When I've run myself down, it takes extra care to get back to my more satisfied and healthy self.

I want to be like Jesus and rest before this happens. After all, Jesus can handle the storms without my help—so I can rest.

MY CONFESSION

I will get some rest today.

What you think you have to do usually can wait.

. . . .

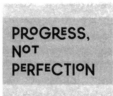

PROGRESS, NOT PERFECTION

Look at your schedule for the upcoming week; what can you cancel or take off your to-do list so you can intentionally get more rest? Do it.

. . . .

God who controls the storms: Thank you for showing me through Jesus the importance of resting. Remind me that I don't have to do everything today. Help me to learn to rest. Amen.

54

WHY REST?

Genesis 1:31–2:3

By the seventh day God had finished the work he had been doing; so on the seventh day he rested from all his work. Then God blessed the seventh day and made it holy, because on it he rested from all the work of creating that he had done.
GENESIS 2:2-3

I'm sure you've heard the rather flippant statement that if God rested, so can we. It's meant to be a vital truth to remind us that God used six days to create the world, including humans, but on the seventh day, God stopped and rested.

Most of us already know the message about Sabbath rest. We know that one day of the week *should* be set aside to remain holy. Some people follow this rule to the tee: no work, no kindling of fire, nothing pertaining to work on the Sabbath. My older cousin once said her mom would fuss at them if they even tried to iron clothes on a Sunday, the day they observed as the Sabbath.

More recently—in our world of go, go, go—I've seen some people interpret Sabbath to mean rest within a day, not just at the end or beginning of the week. They have suggested incorporating rest into each day as a form of self-care.

Regardless of how you observe your Sabbath (weekly or daily), I'm here to add to the thinking that rest *should* be done—regularly, well, and as a priority. Only during the time of the pandemic of 2020 and beyond did I find the peace and comfort of *not* working on the weekends. I've worked a full-time job and side gigs for most of my career. Some of it is normalcy, some of it is trying to catch up on bills or needing extra to fund a desire, and some of it is I just like a nice mix of work. But telling myself to turn off my computer on Saturdays and Sundays gave me such a newfound passion for my work on Monday that I realized I was short-circuiting my creativity by *not* giving my mind and body and soul time to fully rest.

So, as a gift to myself, I try to plan as many no-work weekends as possible. Sometimes deadlines call—but other times they can wait (I'll be better for it on Monday). During these times, I've had to learn to be comfortable with *not doing*. I've had to have some fun hobbies lying around in the cut (to release me from boredom) and a few good books awaiting. I use the time to play games with my family and to try to be fully engaged when I talk on the phone to loved ones. It's a practice that I believe has helped my well-being; it's a practice that is biblical. Try it. Repeat it. Enjoy it and see if it helps with your blues.

MY CONFESSION

I will honor God and my mind through regular Sabbath rests.
Rest is holy.

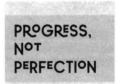

PROGRESS, NOT PERFECTION

Plan your next Sabbath rest; how long will you take? What excuses do you need to overcome?

God of rest: I know you've created Sabbaths to give me time to rest and reconnect with you. Help me put away my excuses and pursue regular, good rest in your name. Amen.

55

THE PROMISE OF MORNING

Psalm 30:1–5

For his anger lasts only a moment, but his favor lasts a lifetime; weeping may stay for the night, but rejoicing comes in the morning.

PSALM 30:5

One of the toughest parts of depression for me was recognizing that the morning didn't always feel fresh and new. As a morning person, I had come to love the early hours of the day. At my healthiest points, mornings are when I get things done. I've written books in the morning (I'm writing at 4 a.m. now!). I've finished projects in the morning. I've cleaned and cooked in the morning. I just feel more inspired and rested early in the day. I know some people are night owls, but I rarely think of something new or good after 7 p.m.—I'm just too tired or I'm in chill mode, desiring to kick back and watch TV, read a book, or go to bed!

So, when mornings started to become a real drag for me—I knew I had a problem. When pulling the covers over my head seemed more fitting than springing out of bed, I knew something was off. When eight hours of sleep turned into nine and sometimes even ten (yet I didn't feel rested), I recognized the signs of depression—and I still do watch out for the morning blues as a symptom.

But I cling to the beautiful imagery David writes about in Psalm 30—morning, true morning, will bring joy; "rejoicing comes in the morning" (v. 5). Yes, weeping may come at night, in the dark times, during the days I want to pull the covers over my head and just stay in bed. But just as the sun sets and dark covers the earth, the sun also rises and fills the land with light. Night is a set period of time. Darkness stays for a moment, but when I'm down and out, I recall that there is the hope of morning. Just as I feel drastically different at nighttime, I know I am refreshed in the morning—and I wait on that time. It helps me get through the dark so I can rejoice when morning rises in my spirit.

Call out to the Lord for help—and look for morning, hope for morning, expect morning. And don't forget to rejoice when it comes.

MY CONFESSION

I will hope and look for morning when my darkness has dissipated. *Morning feels fresh and new; it's a time to rejoice.*

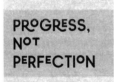

PROGRESS, NOT PERFECTION

Think about the last time you felt renewed. Describe how you felt. Pray for strength to hold out until your morning comes again.

Dear Lord: I wait for morning. I want to feel renewed and refreshed. Remind me that night only lasts for a while. Help me to wait and hope for the new day. Amen.

Bᴇ STILL
Psalm 46:7–11

He says, "Be still, and know that I am God; I will be exalted
among the nations, I will be exalted in the earth."
PSALM 46:10

One of my good friends absolutely dislikes Psalm 46:10. She cringes every time she hears it. (Dare I say her honesty is probably healthy, but I'll discuss that thought in another devotion.) She doesn't want to be still and wait, and she knows herself well enough to know that this isn't her strong suit. However, when she hears the Word of God, she takes it pretty seriously, so this Scripture punctures her heart in particular and reminds her to seek patience as she finds stillness.

I believe stillness is a reminder to sit in God's presence. It's a reminder to quit striving and worrying and trying to bring about change (for now) and to sit in observation of who God is and all God has done and is capable of doing. "Be still, and know that I am God" is a call for me to stop and to observe God.

As a human, I'm like my friend; I don't want to be still. I want to move and get this thing done or figure it out with my mind and jump to my healing. But at last, I hear this verse and I too am prompted to stop, to be active in my stillness—not jumping to the conclusion but recognizing that God is ultimately in control. Stillness recenters me. Stillness quiets my spirit and gets me in tune with my God. Stillness reminds me of just how big God is and just how small I am. Stillness puts things in perspective.

When I'm suffering with the blues, I may be still or paralyzed by my condition, but being still and focusing on God feels different. It's almost like a checkup or a reminder of my God. So, I remember to take a few moments to be still and to sit and think about God more than my issues. It's a call to exalt God as higher than my issues. After all, He is God.

MY CONFESSION

I will intentionally be still today and reflect on who God is.

"Be still, and know that I am God" is a call to stop and focus on God.

PROGRESS, NOT PERFECTION

Be intentional about sitting still today. What do you observe about God in your stillness?

Exalted God: I know who you are. I praise you and exalt you for being God of all. I intentionally still my heart and mind to observe who you are and all you have done and all you are capable of doing. Amen.

57

THE POWER OF HONESTY

Job 3:20–26

For sighing has become my daily food; my groans pour out like water.
JOB 3:24

My reflection about my friend who openly and honestly cringes every time—literally every time—she hears "Be still, and know that I am God" (Psalm 46:10) has prompted another thought. And it's on honesty. Sharing worship space, education space, and now life journeys with this friend has exposed me to her raw honesty. I actually admire how in touch she is with her feelings and how unapologetic she is about expressing them. Don't get me wrong, she and I have had some tough battles—the people-pleasing side of me that just wants things to go smoothly and look pretty and the rugged honesty of my girl who calls it like it is have clashed on several occasions. But, I've also learned that there is great value in pressing through the "hard" relationships, in learning to accept each other's perspectives and personalities and even taking that information and growing. Whoa!

From my friend, I've picked up on the freedom she has from speaking her mind. Because truth is never far from her heart and even lips, she is much more in touch with her emotions than, say, someone like me, who is searching for the nice way to say it or who is trying very hard not to hurt someone's feelings. Years and years of operating in such a manner (tiptoeing around feelings) can make you stuff down your own feelings; it can make you— okay, me—not fully acknowledge some truths that just need to be known.

Job reminds me of my friend. This faithful, righteous man said out loud what he was thinking. Reading through the chapters in the book of Job, you can't help but hurt for him. He suffered. A lot. And brother Job says what he is feeling; he says what he is experiencing. He laments. He lets it out! And we know how this story ends. Job gets to have an audience with God—after Job has laid out his thoughts, regrets, fears, disdain, and raw emotions.

If Job can scream and rant and yell about his true feelings, why can't we? I bet there's some freedom lying beneath those things we've stuffed away and hidden. I bet there's liberty in being in touch with our feelings and being free to express them. The key: find the friends who will listen and not judge, build the friendships like my friend and I have worked very hard to build so we can say whatever we're thinking and feeling, and utilize those journals to get raw and real about your feelings. Expressing them in honesty can be liberating.

MY CONFESSION

I will practice raw and rugged honesty to get in touch with my feelings.

Expressing your true thoughts can be liberating.

PROGRESS, NOT PERFECTION

Find a space to express yourself freely; consider a friend, a counselor, and your journal.

Holy One: I want to be honest with you and with myself.
Help me uncover the layers that I've created to protect myself.
Give me the space to release and the discernment to know
with whom I can share my honest thoughts. Amen.

58

ACCEPTANCE AND CHANGE
Isaiah 43:18–20

*Forget the former things; do not dwell on the past. See, I am
doing a new thing! Now it springs up; do you not perceive it? I
am making a way in the wilderness and streams in the wasteland.*
ISAIAH 43:18–19

As I prayed for the strength and wisdom to write more on navigating through this sea of tough times known as depression and the blues, I was prompted again and again to address grief. Grief is such a big part of life and it can swallow you up in a hole of darkness for years and years. There's no set time on how much you should mourn the loss of ones you've loved. And as I've said before, around holiday time grief can sometimes sneak up on you out of the blue and confuse you. *Why am I sad? It's Christmas, a favorite holiday. Why am I sad when I'm preparing to spend a special day with family and friends?* A birthday? A favorite time of the year? Whatever it may be, remembering your lost loved one on a special day can conjure up grief.

So, what do you do? I've learned to feel the grief. Sit with it. Write about how I'm feeling. Pray about how I'm feeling. Have a good cry. Have a good laugh. I share memories with my sister or even tell my daughter, who never got to meet my mother, a story. Keeping the memories alive and well is important for dealing with grief.

And another thing I tell myself is to enjoy the new. I don't quite forget the past as God commanded Israel in today's Scripture, but I do remember to focus on the new. Yes, I miss my mother dearly. Yes, I'd love to sit at her feet one more time and enjoy some of her cooking or let her enjoy my child and even meet my husband. But that will not be on this side of earth. I know that. And I have new traditions to make, new family members to tell stories to about my mother. I have friends here right now and I want to create memories with them.

During dark times of grief, I create some reminder of my loved one (like poinsettias, my mom's favorite flower, during Christmas; or wearing her favorite pair of earrings on her birthday). I give myself a moment to reflect and remember and then I share that with others. It's not easy—each year can bring on a different emotion. But I'm committed to living on. I've experienced some good, unconditional love from my mother; I want to continue to give and pass on that love.

MY CONFESSION

I will embrace the new traditions of holidays and special days.

Enjoy the new that is emerging after grief and loss.

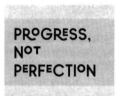

How can you honor your lost loved ones and create new traditions with those who are here?

God of comfort: Send a fresh wave of strength this day as I reflect on the loss of my loved ones. I desire to embrace those who are here with me even as I remember those who are not. Amen.

59

THE SPIRIT OF DEPRESSION
Luke 8:1–3

After this, Jesus traveled about from one town and village to another, proclaiming the good news of the kingdom of God. The Twelve were with him, and also some women who had been cured of evil spirits and diseases: Mary (called Magdalene) from whom seven demons had come out.

LUKE 8:1–2

In my book *Successful Women of the Bible*, I enjoyed diving deeper into the stories of women in the Bible. As I used my research and imagination to fill in some of their unwritten stories and relate them to modern-day women, I was captivated by Mary Magdalene. I've known her as one of the women who discovered Jesus was resurrected (Mark 16:9). I read about her demon possession and even how much she cared for and loved Jesus.

She also comes to mind whenever I hear Christians say we shouldn't be depressed. "We don't have the spirit of depression; we need to pray it off and be grateful." I'd like to hope when people say those things that they are trying to be helpful or cheer up a person who seems down. But I also think they are being insensitive and just don't get how depression works and makes a person feel. There are so many different causes of depression that an outsider can't possibly point out the source. It could be hereditary, chemical, situational (loss of a loved one or job, stress, etc.). It could be something eternal just eating away at you, causing a spirit of sadness to create a cloud over your mind and body.

While I have no idea what was going on with Mary Magdalene, I know she was not well. You can't be if a demon is possessing you. I'm not comparing depression to demon possession but more so looking at how a woman lived and was healed from whatever it was that ailed her—something that had her acting much differently than one who wasn't demon possessed, something that she carried as a label—even centuries later. Her actions while demon possessed must have been newsworthy—because the writers of the Bible didn't leave out that detail.

I won't pretend to give you the cure for depression in this book—neither will you hear me say to "just pray it away." Yes, I will tell you to pray (because I know the power of prayer, and a little talk with Jesus can change a situation!), but I do know the strong hold depression can have on our minds and that it may require more than a prayer. I offer you the example of Mary as a reminder that depression is real and that depression can take over our minds and spirits like other diseases we more readily accept in this country. And sick people—depressed people—need treatment. That may come through psychotherapy, medicine, exercise, a change in circumstances, and, yes, prayer. I believe in all of these treatments and encourage you to seek out what you need.

And I encourage you to follow Mary's example. She was known as the one who had been cured of evil spirits, but she didn't let what people said about her stop her. That was a label others affixed to her. She went on to devote her life to her Healer to follow Him and to support His ministry. She became more than a woman who had several demons living inside of her body, impacting her mental state, no doubt. She became known as one of the first to share the good news.

We are not our conditions. We are not the diseased spirits living inside of our bodies, regardless of the labels people put on us. We are more and we have more to do and more to support—just like Mary.

MY CONFESSION

I am more than the blues. I am a follower of Christ with more to share with the world.

Depression does not define you—even when it feels like it is all-encompassing.

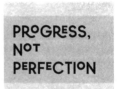

PROGRESS, NOT PERFECTION

Read some of what is written about Mary's story in Mark 16 and Luke 8. How can she be an inspiration for you to keep going?

God of healing: I need you to show up in a mighty way. Direct my steps toward my healing. Give me the strength and courage to seek the help I need to be made whole. Amen.

CHANGING CLOTHES

2 Samuel 12:18–23

Then David got up from the ground. After he had washed, put on lotions and changed his clothes, he went into the house of the LORD and worshiped. Then he went to his own house, and at his request they served him food, and he ate.
2 SAMUEL 12:20

Sometimes when you're deep in despair, covered with darkness, making a small change can make a big difference. I understand that even small, routine tasks seem gigantic and may take a lot of effort, but if you can push yourself to participate in small steps or changes, it may make a difference.

I think about the description of David getting up, washing, putting on lotion, and changing his clothes in 2 Samuel 12:20. He had been fasting and praying and beseeching God about his child. His full focus had been on pleading with God to save his child. When he found out that his child was dead, he got up and made a change. He took care of some basic hygiene and prepared to continue on his way and comfort his wife.

One of my neighbors—who was dealing with a layoff at an older age and was faced with perhaps losing her home because she didn't think she would ever make the income she had made when she was younger—told me what helped her avoid going deeper into depression. She said she got up every day and took a shower and put on clothes. Sometimes she ventured outside of the house for groceries or to care for a loved one, but on other days, she stayed in her home fully dressed. The act of going through a routine helped her. I noticed the value of sticking to a routine when quarantined at home and working remotely during the pandemic. The hot shower felt good and refreshing even though I sometimes thought it would be okay to forgo it and work in my pajamas.

There is something about a routine that can keep us moving and inspired. It may not be the cure for the blues, but it can give us just enough of a push to take another step.

MY CONFESSION

I will get up and take care of routine hygiene each day.

Taking care of your body is important for caring for your mind.

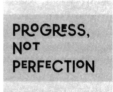

PROGRESS, NOT PERFECTION

Change your clothes; indulge in a long shower; eat your favorite meal.

My God, my Lord: Thank you for a brand-new day. Help me to greet it by taking the routine steps to care for my body even when I don't feel like it. Help me to embrace this new day. Amen.

61

THE POWER OF WATER
John 4:1–14

Jesus answered, "Everyone who drinks this water will be
thirsty again, but whoever drinks the water I give them will
never thirst. Indeed, the water I give them will become in
them a spring of water welling up to eternal life."
JOHN 4:13–14

Throughout the Bible, we see the power of water. In today's passage Jesus is explaining to the woman at the well that He is the living water—what we need to live eternally. I think Jesus chose water as a metaphor because of its significance to life. We need it to live.

Water is also a powerful healing agent. Pools, spas, showers, hot tubs, springs, oceans provide a measure of relief for tired, ailing bodies. I'm sometimes surprised at how refreshed I feel after a hot shower—especially if I've put off taking one for a bit. I also consider it a treat to relax in a tub of water, partly because I never think I have the time to just soak—I have to get in and out to go off to do something else. But, when I remember to treat myself well and just relax in a body of water, I've found relief. Even floating on my back in a pool has brought calmness to my mind and spirit. (It really is one of my best positions to pray in, especially if I'm outside. I can't help but thank God as I look toward the sky and meander down a cool pool.) As I'm submerged in deep water, I feel refreshed and I feel my worries and concerns and blues being released into the depth of the water.

As we deal with the blues, it's important to not forsake some of the basic comforts of life—like water. We may not always consider the healing power of water, but when used regularly and intentionally, it can lift our moods and give us enough hope and inspiration to keep going. The water you need may be in the next room. Try indulging in it as you think of the living water Jesus offered to the woman at the well and to you too. It's able to quench our thirsts and fulfill our needs and desires. Indulge today.

MY CONFESSION

I will enjoy relaxing or indulging in water today.
Water is essential for life; Jesus is the living water.

Indulge in water today. Consider reading a good book or praying while enjoying water.

Living Water: Fall fresh on me this day. As I soak in natural water, remind me of your promise to provide all I need for this life and for eternal life. Help me to be refreshed and renewed by your Holy Spirit. Amen.

62

FOCUSING

Isaiah 26:3–6

You will keep in perfect peace those whose minds are steadfast, because they trust in you.
ISAIAH 26:3

One of the toughest things for me to do on my blue days is to focus. I mean, *really*. First of all, I don't feel like doing anything. Getting out of bed is a challenge. I could just stay right there and pull the covers over my head. But then getting to work and actually doing something productive—that can take a herculean effort.

Here are some things I've learned from years of trying to focus long enough to complete a task when it's extra difficult.

- Acknowledge it's a tough day. Sometimes saying, "It's rough today" (if only to yourself) releases you from the pressures of life. Nothing has changed, but you've taken your temperature and you know what it is.

- Lower the bar. I've already talked about naming what *needs* to get done. Clearly this changes from day to day and based on your responsibilities. Knowing what you absolutely have to get done will help you know what you absolutely *have* to focus on. If your taxes are not due until April 15, stressing about not getting them done on February 1 just doesn't help you during your fragile state. If you get to them, great; if not, you can schedule some time between now and April 15—perhaps on a day you're feeling better—to do them. If you have a deadline for work that is today, use your energy to focus

146

on that—if you cannot get an extension. (Remember, if you were sick with a cold, you'd reach out and probably ask for an extension or take a sick day; mental wellness is as important as physical wellness.) And come to grips with the fact that it will take you longer to get a task completed—because it's just one of those days. Take the pressure off yourself to operate as if things are normal. They are not.

- Know that this is only a day. Your focus may be better tomorrow—or it may get better by the end of the day. Practice breathing, praying, looking for low-hanging fruit today. What can you do that doesn't require all of your focus? Catch up on reading some of the articles your manager sent you? Read the newsletters clogging your mailbox? Or would doing something more active help you out (like making several trips out to the dumpster after you've cleaned your work space)? Whatever it is, try not to get caught up in how badly you feel or how scattered your brain is today.

What is happening right now could be preparing you for your next big idea—your next big breakthrough—or just your next step. You may stumble across something to jump-start you later—sometimes jumping around and *not* focusing inspires a hidden gem.

Take the pressure off yourself. Life continues. Work gets done. Your mind will respond better to gentle care than forced submission. Take good care of yourself—try focusing there for today and learning what that truly means for you during this period. God will grant peace to you when you're steadfast, or focused (see Isaiah 26:3). Sometimes just focusing on the one thing that is important or needs to happen is all you can do.

MY CONFESSION

I will focus on what it means to take good care of myself today.

Focusing on what needs to get done is one way to deal with focus issues when going through the blues.

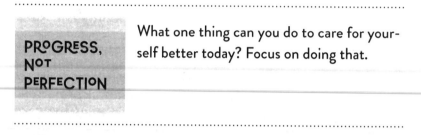

PROGRESS, NOT PERFECTION

What one thing can you do to care for yourself better today? Focus on doing that.

Dear God: It's one of those days. I am having trouble focusing. Give me what I need for this day and help me to remember that you are truly a provider. I know you've given me exactly what I needed before and I trust you will do the same today. Amen.

63

OVERFOCUSING

Proverbs 16:2–4

Commit to the LORD whatever you do,
and he will establish your plans.

PROVERBS 16:3

And just as with most things, there is an additional principle for navigating the blues that seems the opposite of another principle. We looked at focusing in the previous devotional reflection; now, let's consider not overfocusing. It's sometimes comical to think about how human beings work; we can move from one end of a spectrum to the other in a matter of moments. At one point, we can't focus—we're scattered and all over the place, just trying to get one thing completed, yet we're distracted by the least little thing around. Then, if you're anything like me, there are times when we're so focused on a goal that we don't see anything else. And that too can lead to the blues.

This overfocusing happens to me mostly during deadline days or when I want to accomplish a goal and have conjured up enough energy to be dogmatic about my goal. This causes my body to tense up, my mind to only be able to think about finishing or completing my goal, and it makes me miss the beautiful things in life that can refuel me. Dogmatic focus can be a problem.

When I find myself in these modes, I try to stop and breathe and practice all of the reminders I've set up and stored in my mind. *Enjoy the journey. It will get done. Take a break. Breathe.*

I even caution myself about overshooting. If my goal is to write two devotions today, I stop at two instead of going for three or four. Sometimes the space, the rest, the break will supply me with the needed refreshment to continue. If I just keep moving and going and trying and forcing myself to do more, I will give out. I will not be fresh and able to complete my task with joy. Knowing yourself and what works best for you can help you catch your triggers before you've gone down the road to full-on depression.

MY CONFESSION

I will not make my goal my god. I will take a break and pace myself.

Overfocusing can cause stress and make you miss the things that can refuel you.

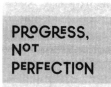

PROGRESS, NOT PERFECTION

Look at your goals for today or the near future. What can you reduce or take off the list to give you the opportunity to breathe?

Creator Lord: Give me the wisdom and strength to pace myself and rest. Help me to remember to refuel to avoid burnout and to be whole and healthy. Amen.

64

TRUTHS TO HOLD ON TO, PART I

Romans 8:37–39

For I am convinced that neither death nor life, neither angels nor demons, neither the present nor the future, nor any powers, neither height nor depth, nor anything else in all creation, will be able to separate us from the love of God that is in Christ Jesus our Lord.

ROMANS 8:38–39

"Snap out of it!" has to be one of the silliest things people can say to loved ones who are depressed or going through a season of the blues. Don't you think the person would click his or her fingers and be released from the fog if they could? Oh, if it were only as easy as clicking our heels together to be back in the land of joy and fun.

But what is helpful for someone going through depression? What can be said? Or more importantly, what can those going through the blues say to themselves? Here's what has helped me—and it's what I keep coming back to when I need a reminder. I call these simple statements my truths to hold on to.

God loves me. That truth never gets old, and sometimes when my mind is distorted by depression, I tend to forget this. Yes, God loves me—even in my depressed state. It's a beautiful realization to know that God loves me no matter how I feel right now. Saying those three words throughout the day—*God loves me*—over and over can help the realization sink into your mind. It can fight back the distorted thoughts depression brings with it. It can remind you that you are worth loving; if God loves you so well, what can you do to love yourself well? How can you take one step toward wholeness today? It may be small—like showering and putting on clothes and simply showing up for the day—or it may be actually doing something you've put off for a while—like looking up your insurance benefits for therapy or counseling or even seeking free options in your community. One step. One way to care for your soul, the soul God loves.

Remind yourself that God's love is great and wide and amazing. Nothing is able to separate us from the mighty power of God's love. And honestly, it's sometimes too much to grasp. But try wrapping your mind around God's love; try looking for ways to feel God's love; try remembering that God's love doesn't change because of what you do or don't do. Embrace God's love for you—regardless of what season you are in.

MY CONFESSION
God loves me; God loves [fill in with your name and repeat].
You can love yourself well because God loves you so well.

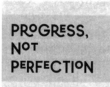

PROGRESS, NOT PERFECTION

Celebrate the one step you make today to love yourself.

God of love: I know you love me and your love is amazing. I know that nothing can separate me from your love. Help me to think of your love throughout the day as I keep moving through this foggy state, one step at a time. Amen.

65

TRUTHS TO HOLD ON TO, PART 2

Genesis 16:7–16

*She gave this name to the LORD who spoke to her:
"You are the God who sees me," for she said, "I have now
seen the One who sees me."*
GENESIS 16:13

Another truth I believe is helpful to hold on to during the deep, dark days of depression is that God sees you. God knows exactly where you are and what you're going through. God sees you—yes, you.

I'm not here to give you medicine for your condition, but I can point to God's Word and our faith story to remind you of the truth. Look at Hagar. If you do not know her story, you can find it in Genesis 16 and 21. For a summary, Hagar was a servant to Abram's (Abraham's) wife, Sarai (Sarah). When Sarah could not conceive, she demanded that her husband sleep with Hagar to produce a child.

And as life would have it, that's exactly what happened. And no one was happy. Hagar despised Sarah and Sarah despised Hagar (Genesis 16:4). Let's just say the conditions in that household were not pretty. So, Hagar ran away—pregnant, distraught, and probably with little hope of a future.

As she sat near a spring in a hot desert, an angel showed up to speak with her. The angel let Hagar in on some news. He told her that the Lord had heard about her condition and that she would indeed have a son (v. 11).

That piece of news from the angel gave Hagar hope. She felt seen by God; she realized God had not forgotten her and God knew exactly what was going on. Her conditions didn't change immediately—the angel told her to go back and submit to Sarah, the one who had started the trouble (v. 9). Yet now she was going back with some truth to hang on to—God knew exactly where she was.

When your days get dark and feel hopeless, try hanging on to the words Hagar spoke: "You are the God who sees me" (v. 13). Take comfort in knowing God sees and God has a plan.

MY CONFESSION

Despite my condition, I will hold on to the truth that God sees me. *God knows exactly where you are and what you need.*

PROGRESS, NOT PERFECTION

Read Hagar's story and try to imagine the emotions she must have felt. What must it have felt like to receive such a message from the angel of the Lord? How can the angel's message help you remember God sees you? Write your thoughts in a journal and revisit them when you need a reminder.

God who sees me: Thank you for the reminder of the truth that you see me. Give me the strength to hang on until my condition changes. Amen.

66

TRUTHS TO HOLD ON TO, PART 3

Hebrews 10:22–24

Let us hold unswervingly to the hope we profess,
for he who promised is faithful.
HEBREWS 10:23

I feel like I should call this section of devotions "What I Know for Sure." It's the things I tie my rope around when I'm uncertain; it's the anchoring statements that I can rest on even when my compass seems to be going haywire. It's the assurances I have regardless of how I'm feeling.

God is faithful.

I know this to be true. I can review my life and see God's hand carrying me through good and bad times. I can see God making a way out of no way—well, no way that I ever thought was possible. I can think about the "surprises" I received throughout my life that helped me catapult past trouble. I can even see the times things could have gone so much worse than they did yet I was spared; somehow I got out of those situations. I may have a few wounds and scrapes and scars, but I can see how God's hand of protection kept me and is still keeping me.

Early on in my marriage, my husband reminded me to always come back to the fact that he loves me. He said I should tie a knot around that truth and use it to work through any other thoughts I was having. (You know how the mind works! When I centered on the fact that my husband loved me, it put the other things in perspective even if it did prompt a discussion or argument.)

God's faithfulness is like that. I can tie my knot around the truth that God does what God says; God protects, provides, and keeps me. The ways He does that may seem different from what I expect, but they are still there.

Review stories of your favorite Bible characters and trace God's faithfulness. Review testimonies of family members and observe God's faithfulness. Review your life story and think of ways God has shown up and shown out—just in time and just for you. God is faithful; this I know full well. God is faithful—I pray you can hold on to that nugget of truth this day as you navigate the blues and expect God's healing power to take over your mind.

MY CONFESSION

God is faithful.

You can know for sure—God is faithful.

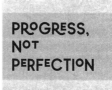

PROGRESS, NOT PERFECTION

Trace God's faithfulness throughout your life. Tie a rope around God's faithfulness to you and repeat this truth over and over to help you get through.

Faithful God: I declare and decree that you truly have been faithful to me. I stand on your promises and I rest in the assurance of knowing you are with me right now even as I walk through this valley. Amen.

67

TRUTHS TO HOLD ON TO, PART 4

Matthew 28:16–20

Surely I am with you always, to the very end of the age.
MATTHEW 28:20

The Great Commission—the departing message Jesus left with His followers—gives us a certainty and a truth we need to cling to for dear life—especially when our minds are distorted from the pressures of life and the blues.

Jesus's words are a promise to us that He is by our side while we finish the work needed on this earth. Jesus told the disciples to go and make more disciples, followers of Him. We are those people, the ones called to follow the way of Jesus. And His promise to abide with the disciples is for us too.

Regardless of how you feel, you are not alone. God walks right by your side. Depression can make you feel all alone; you may even think you're the only person suffering and you may not feel as if there's hope for a better day. I pray the words in this book have opened your eyes to know that that is just a distortion; that is not the truth. You do not suffer alone. God knows and hears your prayers; God knows your condition as well as the help that is needed.

While you seek treatments and tricks to help you keep moving, walk assuredly knowing that God is with you. Hang on to that truth with all you have—so you can make it to the next moment. Talk directly to God; tell Him exactly how you feel; share what you think you need and wait with anticipation for answers.

God's promises are real; God's promises are worth holding on to. He is with you always—until the very end of the age.

MY CONFESSION

I know I am not alone; I will cling to the Lord's promise to be with me.

You are never alone and God always delivers on His promises.

PROGRESS, NOT PERFECTION

Walk throughout this day talking to God, remembering that you are not alone.

Faithful God: I'm so grateful for all of your promises. I know I'm not alone even when I feel like I am. Help me to walk and talk with you throughout this day. Amen.

68

IF GOD HAS DONE IT BEFORE . . .

Matthew 19:25–27

Jesus looked at them and said, "With man this is impossible, but with God all things are possible."
MATTHEW 19:26

In the midst of depression, it can be helpful to hold on to the truths you know, the undisputable knowledge you've gained throughout the years. As I've said before, depression can distort your thoughts. You're prone to exaggerate things because of the way you feel. It's tough to see a way out because of the distortions. But holding on to the things you know that you know regardless of how you are feeling right now can get you through.

Some of the most helpful truths I hold on to have come from music—because I play music on those cloudy days even though I don't always want to. The act of turning on music or turning to my playlist is an act of protest against the spiritual battle I'm fighting against the blues (try it!). Digesting truths I know to be certain even with a distorted view gives me hope and inspiration and a reminder that things are not going to feel cloudy forever.

In his upbeat hit "If He Did It Before," Tye Tribbett belts out that God is the same God who did many miracles in the lives of those in the Bible as well as in our lives today. He's reminding me that if God was capable of healing the sick before, He's more than capable of healing me too. If God has lifted my head from depression before, I know God is able to do it again. This song becomes my proclamation to give me hope for brighter days.

Jesus himself told His followers that some things seem impossible for human beings, and in times of deep depression, healing definitely feels elusive and impossible. We have no idea how or when our balm will come to soothe our pain. But the end of today's Scripture verse points back to the God we serve; *all things* are possible with Him. Therefore, I can wait on my healing; I can anticipate my healing even through help from those God has provided, and through discernment He has given me about things I can do for wellness and wholeness. This healing is not impossible, for I know God has done it before and will do it again.

MY CONFESSION

I know all things are possible with God.
Sometimes truths to hold on to come from the lyrics in music.

PROGRESS, NOT PERFECTION

Listen to Tye Tribbett's song "If He Did It Before." Create a list of the "impossible" things God has done in your life.

Loving God: I declare that all things are possible with you.
I look back over my life and I give you thanks for all of the many times you have brought me through. I stand on my faith in you right now. Amen.

PURPOSE IN TODAY
Psalm 118

This is the day which the LORD hath made;
we will rejoice and be glad in it.
PSALM 118:24 KJV

One thing I've learned while fighting through depression—and then reflecting back on those cloudy days even through writing this book—is that depression makes me magnify everything. And that applies particularly to the way I feel. *My symptoms are the absolute worse. I won't feel better any time soon. I can't possibly do anything. I don't even know how I'm functioning right now.*

Geez, that voice inside your head will send you down a rabbit hole—and quickly. But a lyric from a Kirk Franklin song has stuck in my head and surfaced especially on those days I think are the worst and want to just erase from my life (mind you, not because of any tragedy but because of the exaggerated way I feel at the moment). I caught this quick lyric in the midst of a nice, upbeat song with a great message to help you get through the day. Ironically, when I searched for that phrase, it's not even listed in all the lyrics; it may be an add-on in some versions— that's how elusive the phrase was. But one day, at the right time, I caught it and it has stayed in my spirit and mind and given me the needed push especially on those really hard days.

In "Smile" by Kirk Franklin, in some versions he says in the middle of the music that every day won't be perfect like you'd like it, but even in those days there can be purpose. I've taken those words to mean every minute or moment doesn't have to be perfect either. Lord knows nothing feels close to perfect when your mind is distorted and in a depressed state. But it also doesn't mean I need to throw away the day or even the moment. Something could be happening here to show me how to keep going; something could be happening here to help someone else down the line; something could be happening—even in the mundane, depressed, numb state I am currently in.

Don't discount today just because you don't feel like it's perfect or you don't feel well. There can still be purpose emerging from the feelings that accompany the blues. The scene could be forming for a story you haven't realized you're telling. That's one of the beauties of God; you don't always know what God is up to, but you can trust that He is moving and working—even when you feel your worst. This day can have some purpose—regardless of how you feel about it. Don't discount what is happening right now to bring about wholeness and wellness. Walk through the process knowing that Someone bigger than you is working and is in control. Remind yourself of this truth throughout the day and see if you can find purpose—and a reason to rejoice—in this day.

MY CONFESSION

There is purpose even in this day and even if I don't see it.

Don't discount what is happening today to produce wholeness and wellness in spite of how you feel.

PROGRESS, NOT PERFECTION

Try reflecting on all God has done that you may give Him praise for today. Read Psalm 118 for inspiration.

PURPOSE IN TODAY

Almighty and merciful God: Thank you for this day and all it holds. Even when I don't feel well, I know you are in control and able to work through me this day. Thank you for always having a plan and making a way. Amen.

A PLEA TO GOD

Psalm 38

LORD, do not forsake me; do not be far from me, my God.
Come quickly to help me, my Lord and my Savior.
PSALM 38:21-22

Sometimes I have to just shake my head when I think of all of the times I've heard Christians say things about depression I strongly disagree with. I could repeat some of those things right now, but I'm sure you've heard them before (and I've listed some in this book already).

But what I don't understand is how these people who speak out against depression and say we should never be downtrodden or blue or filled with anxiety can explain some of the verses in the Bible—spoken by people of faith. Like today's psalm. Beware, if you read the entirety of Psalm 38, you get weighed down. It's heavy. Goodness! And these words are from the mouth of David, a beloved man of faith whom we know God made and kept many promises to—particularly that his family would reign on the throne of Israel forever. (And that is fulfilled through our gift of Christ. Amen! See 2 Samuel 7:13.)

In this psalm, David is in a bad way. None of my commentaries say exactly what has happened, but David is pouring out his heart to the Lord. David is in anguish. He's repenting from some sin and guilt—something we should all do regularly (not that our depression is automatically tied to sin, but it sure can't hurt to come clean to God and others). He sounds like his emotional state has impacted his body (as he says his "back is filled with searing pain"; Psalm 38:7). You do know our emotions can have an impact on our bodies—which is another reason we should press toward healing and wholeness. Too many times we're carrying around the anguish for too many years and it is directly related to some of our other health challenges. And we then find ourselves in a cycle—we're depressed because of our emotions, which then has an impact on our body, which then makes us more blue.

In this psalm, David feels mute and deaf. He feels as if his words are falling on deaf ears—even his friends have turned their backs on him. He is misunderstood—even though he tries to do good. It's rough and it's tough, yet even after all of the feelings he expresses throughout this psalm, David reminds us of what we also should hang on to in the midst of deep darkness. It's a truth David knew full well; it's a truth we know as well. God is still available to us in the midst of our dark hole. Cry out and ask Him not to forsake you—even if you feel forsaken. Ask God to come quickly and provide what you need to keep moving forward.

Until then—know that you're not alone; you are actually in good company. Some great people of faith have endured some really tough and dark moments—and they've made it through. You can too.

MY CONFESSION

I can make it through the dark night.

People of faith suffer from depression.

PROGRESS, NOT PERFECTION

Read Psalm 38. How do you identify with David?

NAVIGATING THE BLUES

Lord and Savior: Send help quickly. I need you now. Give me exactly what I need so I may press through this moment of darkness and be made whole. Amen.

ONE STEP AT A TIME
Matthew 6:9–14

Give us today our daily bread.
MATTHEW 6:11

Whether you love Tyler Perry or not—whether you think his movies are ridiculous or whether you've found some comedic relief from Madea—I have received some major inspiration from his productions, particularly his movie *Diary of a Mad Black Woman*, starring Shemar Moore and Kimberly Elise.

I watched this movie once during a stretch of depressed weeks (or months). I'm not sure if I was down because of circumstances or if it was one of those blue moments that lasted longer than normal. What I do know is I was alone in my apartment watching the story of all of the tumultuous trouble Kimberly Elise's character Helen seemed to go through. Her husband cheated on her, her husband treated her like trash, and then her husband divorced her. She struggled to find herself and her strength after having clung so tightly to the fairy tale she had built in her mind.

Somehow, through the help of her grandmother Madea and her mother (played by the amazing Cicely Tyson), prayer, and writing in her diary, Helen pieced together her life and mustered up the strength to get a job, support herself, and move on. During the scene that struck me, she was writing in her diary and she said most days she didn't want to get out of bed. "Some people say one day at a time—seems too long for me. Most days all I can do is moment to moment."

I could have shouted right there as if I were in a worship service. (It didn't hurt that the soundtrack was on point and in the next scene she ran into Shemar Moore's character again!) But seriously, Helen was right. One day at a time may seem too long when we're underwater and drowning in our blues. Sometimes we just have to take it moment by moment. Focus on one moment at a time.

Depression can distort your thinking so that you become so overwhelmed with all that seems to be up against you. How will you do this or that? You can do it just like Elise's character and just like me: one step at a time, moment by moment.

One of my coworkers had a proverb displayed in her office: "How do you eat an elephant? One bite at a time." This saying always reminded me that I needed to take things one step at a time. Sometimes those steps look like getting out of bed and doing the bare minimum required. Other days those steps look like seeking help or taking a walk or even organizing a cabinet that has been bothering you for the longest time, or creating a welcoming work space to help you get through your creative dry spells.

Give yourself grace to take it one step at a time. Pray to God for help knowing what that step is and inhale and exhale as you move closer to being able to accomplish that task. Don't worry about the next; trust me, it will be there. For this day, may God grant you what you need to make it one step at a time.

MY CONFESSION

I will take one step at a time.

How do you eat an elephant? One bite at a time.

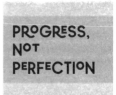

PROGRESS, NOT PERFECTION

Find a saying, a meditation, to remind you to take things one step at a time.

Heavenly God: I will take things one step at a time today. I will not focus on tomorrow. Show me the next step and help me to appreciate this day. Amen.

72

GOD'S WILL
Psalm 84:10–12

For the LORD God is a sun and shield; the LORD bestows
favor and honor; no good thing does he withhold from
those whose walk is blameless.

PSALM 84:11

I found today's verse tucked away in a psalm during a particularly challenging period in my life. I had been praying about something so much that I probably stopped praying for it. (You know how some prayers become such a part of who you are that you're not sure when you stopped asking God for your desires?) Well, this verse spoke to me because it says that God will not withhold a good thing from me. So in my natural mind, I thought that would mean I should have all the good things I desired.

I wrestled with this verse for a while because I'm also old enough to know that you just don't get everything you pray for (which can be a blessing too). But deep down as I wrestled with depression—and still do wrestle with it—I can't help but think that a whole mind and soul is a good thing *and* the will of God. I don't think God wants me depressed and wrestling with anxiety. I don't think the blues are a good thing, but I do think a cure must be a good thing.

So, when I'm wrestling, wondering, *How long, dear Lord,* and working through all of the various forms of help available during these days, I keep this verse in mind. I don't have the answers and Lord knows I don't have the cure, but knowing that God doesn't withhold good things from me gives me hope. I'm not blameless, but I am forgiven because of my belief in Christ.

This verse reminds me to not count myself out of the fight because there's a good thing developing even in the midst of what feels so bad. I believe that wholeness is available. I believe that wholeness is the will of God and I will keep seeking healing and help during the tough seasons.

I repeat constantly: *No good thing will He withhold from me.* I look for the good in the midst of the tough and I wait. And I pray. And I expect wholeness and healing. I take God's word to heart.

MY CONFESSION

I believe that wholeness is a good thing.
No good thing will God withhold.

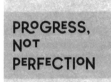

PROGRESS, NOT PERFECTION

List the good things God has not withheld from you in the past. Use your list to give you hope in healing.

Healer God: I expect to be made whole and healed. Show me the ways you've made for me to receive healing as I deal with this challenge. Amen.

73

BOREDOM AND THE BLUES
Romans 8:12–17

This resurrection life you received from God is not a timid, grave-tending life. It's adventurously expectant, greeting God with a childlike "What's next, Papa?" God's Spirit touches our spirits and confirms who we really are. We know who he is, and we know who we are: Father and children. And we know we are going to get what's coming to us—an unbelievable inheritance! We go through exactly what Christ goes through. If we go through the hard times with him, then we're certainly going to go through the good times with him!

ROMANS 8:15–17 MSG

A friend once said a group of loving and caring friends had some helpful advice when he was going through his own bout of blues. (Yes, sometimes people can be helpful; take what works best for you and leave the rest. Most people do want what's best for you, even if they don't know how to talk to you during your roughest times.)

This friend said his wise friends told him he needed something to look forward to. They were basically sensing that their friend's blues stemmed from the boredom that can creep in when we're living life and going about the routine, monotonous tasks we have to do. Sometimes in life we can be so focused on just making it through the day, getting through the right now—working, caring for others, completing school, getting a job, and more—that we become all consumed with the now. We lose our hope and desire for other things. We lose the excitement that is also a part of life.

I turn to *The Message* version of Romans 8 for inspiration. I love the imagery of me saying, "What's next, Papa?" as if I'm awaiting a new adventure, a new experience, and a new journey. And it's not a journey I'm taking alone. I'm asking God what is next. I'm envisioning God as my "cruise director" who is really in control of my life and has some things planned for me. Now, I'm old enough to know all of these adventures may not seem like fun at first—but with God they can truly be an adventure. The focal point for me is that I'm with God. I'm journeying through life with someone bigger and better than me—and there's some excitement packed away in just the journey. So, as I go about completing the regular, normal, day-to-day tasks I have before me, I also look around the corner and ask my Papa what's next. What adventures lie ahead that I may miss if I don't have an expectant attitude? What do I need to open my eyes and heart to? Could it be just the next person I meet or serve? Or could it already be here, awaiting my mind and spirit to catch up?

What are you looking forward to? Can it be today's task or something in the future? It's a great idea to always have something to look forward to—and to keep your eyes and ears and heart open to what adventure God may take you on next.

MY CONFESSION
I have plenty to look forward to. I'm on a journey with God.
Find occasions to anticipate and look forward to in the future.

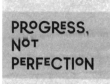

PROGRESS, NOT PERFECTION

Start your list. What are you looking forward to? Remember, it can be something very small, like a day off, or something huge, like an upcoming family wedding or trip. How will you make sure God is directing the journey?

God of my past, present, and future: Give me eyes to look forward to not only what you have planned for me in eternity but what is around the corner. Help me to anticipate good days of fellowship and fun. Amen.

74

MEMºIRS

Psalm 107:1–3

Let the redeemed of the LORD tell their story—those he
redeemed from the hand of the foe.
PSALM 107:2

In the publishing world just a few years ago, it seemed as if we were bombarded with books in a genre known as memoir. Everyone was looking back over their lives and sharing stories about things that happened to them. Famous people as well as those who didn't have a big following were reviewing their lives and telling their stories. When I started a longer commute, I turned to Audible for a few audiobooks to help time pass on my long drives and in traffic. (Side note: I also looked forward to an autobiographical rendering from a famed person on my walks; it made me want to walk when I knew I had someone waiting to tell me a story.)

So, as I listened to some famous people rewind and reflect on their lives, I did the same. Their stories about their births or significant moments when they were children made me think about my birth narrative: What were my mother and father thinking when I was born? What messages did I receive about my birth throughout my childhood? These stories helped me process why I think the way I think, why I react the way I react, and what I needed to work on to identify triggers and moments that could lead down a path of more problematic mental concerns.

I encourage you to think about your own memoir—whether you'll actually write and publish it or not. Ask yourself some of the questions the famous people are asking as they uncover parts of their past. What significant stories shape you?

Some of the stories you turn up will not be joyous, I'm certain. And you may need help to navigate through them in a healthy way, but I do think the journey will be helpful. When you put in the hard work you may uncover reasons that have led to your feeling blue or sad or being triggered by certain things or events at certain times of the year. Getting to know yourself better can be a healthy by-product of navigating through the road of depression. It can open doors to your soul that have been locked. Your imprisoned soul may need to be free. The things locked away may need to be cleared out and replaced with tools to assist your well-being.

MY CONFESSION

I will reflect on my life to become healthy and well.

Our stories help to shape who we are and how we see ourselves and the world.

....

PROGRESS, NOT PERFECTION

What are some significant stories that have shaped you? Remember and reflect.

....

God of my silent years: I know you know all about me and my life. As I reflect on my years, give me the wisdom and discernment to deal with the stories that make up my life in a healthy manner to produce wellness. Amen.

75

THE TRUTH WILL SET YOU FREE

John 8:27–33

Then you will know the truth,
and the truth will set you free.
JOHN 8:32

The suggestion of thinking through what would be in your memoir may not be the easiest exercise for many. Our pasts can have some dark holes and some places we'd just rather not revisit. But I've found one of the salves for dealing with my inner turmoil is that learning more about myself—speaking honestly about my fears, perceived failures, background, family, regrets, and so on—is helpful for maintaining a healthy well-being. Saying what I truly feel and think helps expose some things that may cause unhealthy behaviors. When you can look deep inside yourself—without lying or trying to cover up what you may think is shameful—you can hopefully face some realities.

This is not a judgment zone; there's no room for the negative, self-condemning thoughts that can sometimes come from looking within. This time, remind yourself that this truth-searching venture is meant to help you and to free you. You're not strolling down memory lane to find someone to blame, including yourself. You want to know why you react the way you do and why you think the way you do. It's not even necessarily time for change; acknowledgment is the first step to confronting some good, bad, and even ugly things.

As scary as the truth is, know that it can set you free. And freedom is beautiful and liberating—and a great path toward healing.

MY CONFESSION
I want to be free.
Looking inside can uncover the truth and set you free.

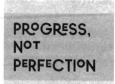

PROGRESS, NOT PERFECTION

What steps do you need to take to help you uncover truths? Start today.

God of truth: I desire to know more about myself and all that has impacted me. Give me strength to do the hard work of uncovering truth on this journey toward liberation. I want to be free. Amen.

76

THESE EMOTIONS

Ecclesiastes 7:8–10

Do not be quickly provoked in your spirit,
for anger resides in the lap of fools.
ECCLESIASTES 7:9

Emotions can be a funny thing. I've been working on managing mine as I learn to navigate through the blues. This has been a life-long task, filled with plenty of starts and stops. Life's circumstances (like stress or a pandemic) as well as life's milestones (perimenopause for me) can make emotions fluctuate. But, I know I have to keep trying to deal with my emotions. I desire to be my healthiest in my mind and body. I exercise and try to make good food choices for the physical part; I even take medicine daily for some of my physical diagnoses so I can become and remain healthy.

I know I need to exercise some of the same discipline and faithfulness for my mental state (and dare I say we as a society need to make mental health a priority as high as physical health at least). Managing those emotions is a big part of being mentally healthy. By managing, I mean being able to stop and reflect about what has caused the emotion I am currently experiencing. Now, this doesn't take away the emotion—if I'm angry, it will take more than identifying the culprit or stimulus to calm me down. But what identifying the culprit does is help me channel my energy toward that circumstance. I can ask myself if there's anything I can do right now to alleviate the issue. If so, I can do that. If not, I can think of other ways to handle the emotion in the immediate present and in the future. And I can set up a plan—either formally or in my mind—to take steps to get toward my solution. I know I won't always be able to solve things quickly—some things will have to be lived with, which is also a part of managing my emotions.

I know when I don't manage my emotions, I take actions and I have to deal with the consequences of those actions. I've had enough angry releases where I've said (and even done) things I regret. I know not dealing with my emotions when they creep up results in negative reactions. Yet, it is still a challenge each day I have emotions (uhm, every day). And anger stays around only in the lap of fools, says the wise teacher in Ecclesiastes. Anger is not meant to hang out long term in our bodies and minds; when it does, it can make us even more depressed or blue. Not dealing with our anger in a healthy manner has worse consequences than we sometimes know.

Are you checking in with yourself regularly—several times a day—to see how you are feeling and what you are feeling and perhaps tying it to a stimulus? It's an exercise worth trying to help make and keep you mentally healthy.

MY CONFESSION

I will continue to work on managing my emotions.

Managing emotions involves being able to stop and reflect on what caused the emotion to surface.

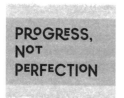

PROGRESS, NOT PERFECTION

Check in with yourself regularly today.
What emotion are you experiencing? Why?

Dear Lord: I want to be healthy and whole. Help me to identify the source of my emotions so that I may deal with them in a healthy way. I know you are able to help me. Amen.

GOOD CHANGE

Proverbs 27:7–12

*The prudent see danger and take refuge, but the simple
keep going and pay the penalty.*
PROVERBS 27:12

While seeking to manage your emotions and employing various mental health tools, I also think it is important to not underestimate the toll change takes on the body. Many of us have considered how we age and change physically, but what about circumstances of life and how they impact us? Even good change can cause a shift in emotions and well-being.

At my first full-time job, the human resources director shared with me the importance of making room for this type of emotion related to good change. She reviewed all the changes I had experienced within a small amount of time. She rattled off: "You've graduated from school. You've relocated to a new city and state. You've started a new job. That's a lot of change. Don't forget to take extra care of yourself during this time; don't discount the impact of good change."

As she shared what she knew about my changes, I was kind of surprised. She was right; I had undergone some major changes, including some things she didn't even know about. Even when desired and sought after, changes like these contribute to major stress and emotional fluctuation. When we don't stop and take special care during these times of change—even good change— the emotional result can sneak up on us.

Here's where the practice of regular check-ins can help you. Once a week or month (even every day if you can), stop and ask yourself how you are doing, how you are feeling, what is stimulating your current emotions. How can you make sure you acknowledge all you are going through and have gone through, and give yourself the needed care? Prudent people, says Proverbs, take stock of where they are and assess what is needed.

Don't forget to care for yourself through the good and the bad; change happens. Change is inevitable and so are the emotions that come along with shifts in our lives.

MY CONFESSION

I will check in with myself to monitor my emotions especially during times of change.

Change is inevitable—even good change.

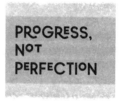

PROGRESS, NOT PERFECTION

Practice checking in with yourself and your emotions. When you feel an emotion arise, stop and reflect on what caused the emotion and how you can proceed in a healthy manner.

Heavenly Father: Remind me to be gentle with myself especially during times of change, even good change. Help me to hang on to your unchanging hand and recognize you as my only constant in life. Amen.

78

CHALLENGE DAYS

Romans 12:1–8

Do not conform to the pattern of this world, but be transformed by the renewing of your mind. Then you will be able to test and approve what God's will is—his good, pleasing and perfect will.
ROMANS 12:2

A few years ago, it seems internet challenges began. It could have been social media's "viralness" that caused us all to take on a challenge. We went from pouring water on ourselves to thirty days of squats. Challenges for everything surfaced as a way to help us pick up some healthy habits and stick to them for at least thirty days.

I'd love to propose another challenge—one I've taken with myself often when trying to wrangle my emotions to a healthy place. I challenge myself to see something different or new each day. I challenge myself to turn negative thoughts around immediately when they creep up in my head. I challenge myself to have a thankful Tuesday (or Thursday) and purposefully name out loud my blessings; looking for things to be thankful for forces me to acknowledge many things I take for granted. Oh, that running water; oh, the car to drive, the child to take care of, the money to pay the bills that are due. Yep, these challenges can stretch you and they are meant to do that. They are also meant to force you to think differently. Focusing on shifting your thoughts can be enough to get you through the day; for a period of time, you're not focusing on how numb you feel or down you are, but instead you're trying to find beauty in this day or count blessings or shift to positivity.

You can create your own challenge for whatever amount of time you choose. Pick something to focus on that's a challenge to you and run with it. Get creative and enjoy pushing yourself to see things differently today. If you don't make it, it's okay. Try again tomorrow. Alter your challenge. Don't give up. If you make it, well, you have just another thing to be proud of and to feel you've accomplished—and you've made it through another day, perhaps with more gratitude in your heart and more awareness of your surroundings. Take the win where you can get it—especially when navigating through the blues. And don't forget to celebrate—we can so often kick ourselves when we're down, when a little celebration can go a long way. What is your challenge for this day?

MY CONFESSION

I will challenge myself to _____ today.
Focusing on shifting your thoughts can be a challenge worth pursuing.

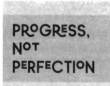

Make a plan to fulfill your challenge today. Check on your progress throughout the day.

God of all: Give me new eyes to see challenges as an opportunity to push forward and shift my mind. I want to _____ [fill in with your challenge]. Help me and guide me. Amen.

79

RITUALS
Luke 22:14–20

And he took bread, gave thanks and broke it, and gave it to them, saying, "This is my body given for you; do this in remembrance of me."
LUKE 22:19

As Christians we are familiar with the sacrament known as Communion in many churches. It's the time set aside to regularly recall the sacrifice of Jesus Christ. We take bread, which symbolizes Christ's body that was broken for you and for me; we drink wine or juice to reflect on the precious blood of Jesus that was shed just so you and I could be forgiven for our sins. What a beautiful gift of grace it is to commemorate what Jesus has done for us—as often as we can.

The ritual of Communion reminds me of the significance of many different rituals. We do them routinely—and to be quite honest, sometimes mindlessly. We know they are good for us (usually) and we do them because we're just used to doing them. We have done them so often that we don't need to think very hard about them. Brushing our teeth, making our bed, even praying. These are things we do without needing to think very hard.

During periods of depression, I believe it's important to keep those rituals going. Even if you feel like you don't get much out of them, do them anyway. First of all, they give your life a sense of normalcy; when you're spiraling out of control, a routine can provide a level of comfort that you may not even be aware of. And continue to pray and seek God—regardless of how you feel. Say your prayers at the same time each day—even written or memorized ones like the Lord's Prayer. Be consistent, be faithful—even when it's hard to focus and get your mind into the routine. Scripture reminds us that the Holy Spirit can pray for us too by interpreting our groans—so the words don't have to come (see page 198).

Another reason to perform rituals is because their meaning reminds you of how things should be. My prayers to God don't mean everything is all right; they remind me that I'm praying to the One who can make things all right. My repeating Scripture doesn't mean everything is fixed, but it reminds me of the One who can fix things and who has fixed things in the past. Your mind and body will begin to adapt to your ritual—it's what you do. And these rituals can help you when you just don't feel it.

MY CONFESSION

I will follow a ritual today.

Rituals remind us of how things should be.

PROGRESS, NOT PERFECTION

Write down at least two rituals you will make a part of your everyday life. Do them.

Lord of all: I thank you for all you've done in the past, particularly the giving of Christ for my sins. Help me to use rituals to recall your faithfulness as I navigate through this period. Amen.

HELP SOMEONE

Galatians 6:1–6

*Carry each other's burdens, and in this way
you will fulfill the law of Christ.*
GALATIANS 6:2

As I've journeyed through life dealing with depression, reading many articles, and just paying attention to the way we treat mental illness as well as what people say to those dealing with the blues, I've heard some pretty controversial and insensitive things. In Christian circles especially I've heard that we should just get out of ourselves and help someone else. Quit thinking about your issues and focus on someone else's—I guess that's what they mean.

But it's in this advice that I find extremely insensitive and uninformed that I also find a remnant of help. The insensitivity and ignorance first: Why would you think knowing someone else has issues helps my issues? Blues, depression, anxiety come for a variety of reasons—and sometimes they cannot even be linked to a reason. And there are treatments for depression, not cures. Releasing our judgment—even for ourselves—about why we are depressed can assist us in granting compassion to not only ourselves but those around us who are struggling. Releasing our false ideas about cures rather than treatments may give us the compassion needed to make it another day and take more steps toward wholeness rather than recoiling in shame.

But on to the good stuff: the remnant in that advice to get outside of yourself. While helping others won't take away your issues and struggles, it can help you when dealing with your blues. You see, throwing yourself into caring for others reminds you that you have purpose. Your care could help someone by tangibly meeting a need or it could put a smile on someone else's face. That can transfer to you and give you a smile, even if for a moment. And, yes, it reminds you that we're all just trying to make it in this world—knowing you're not out here alone is helpful. While comparing struggles is not helpful, meeting a need and sharing in a tangible solution can be.

And I'll be honest, when my thoughts are distorted, I can sometimes only think about how awful I feel, and I can begin to lose hope about when and how I will feel better or reach wellness. Getting out and focusing elsewhere (for even a short period of time) can help you and someone else. That's a win-win and one of our missions as followers of Christ. Carrying another's burdens is caring. Carrying another's burdens is Christlike.

MY CONFESSION

I will look for a tangible way to help someone else today.

Helping others can help you—even if just for a moment.

....

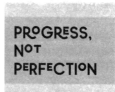

Just do it. Help someone today.

....

Heavenly Father: Open my eyes to the needs of others around me. Give me the will and strength and capacity to help someone today. Amen.

DON'T GIVE UP
Galatians 6:7–10

Let us not become weary in doing good, for at the proper time we will reap a harvest if we do not give up.
GALATIANS 6:9

I'm a habitual dieter. Well, let me say this: I've been a habitual dieter. I'm changing my mindset and having success at that—as well as changing the words I use to describe my habits. You see, throughout my adult life—perhaps even my childhood—I've reached for food when I'm feeling sad, angry, stressed, joyful; they call this emotional eating. And after I'd suffered with depression silently for many years, you can imagine what that emotional eating did to my weight and more importantly my health. But I've found some nugget of truth and help in each diet I have attempted. And one of the lessons I learned on one particular diet was to not give up. When you eat off your plan, don't just throw in the towel and continue to eat off the plan, which for me led to bingeing and probably regaining what I had lost and more. No, I needed to treat that moment when I fell off the wagon as just that: a moment. Under my new mindset, I'm realizing that eating well and making the right choices is a lifestyle, not a diet plan. I want to make healthy choices for the rest of my life—not the three weeks I've committed to an eating plan or paid my money for a seminar or way to track food.

And you know what? Being committed to this wholeness movement, where I want to be healthy mentally too, takes the same mindset. I can't quit. I can't stop striving for wholeness and wellness. If I have a bad moment, I need to treat it as just that: a bad moment. Perhaps I've slipped into an old, unhelpful habit; perhaps I feel like I'm in a pit that I can't crawl out of. But when I have the mindset to not give up, I will continue to take one step at a time and do what I know is good—good for my mind, body, and soul; good for my emotions; good for my wellness.

The verse for today is usually applied to people helping each other—and that's good, for the writer says that we should do good to all people (Galatians 6:10). Today, I challenge you to also apply doing good to yourself and to your mind and to your body. Don't get tired when it's hard to put into practice some of the routines and rituals and habits that we've discussed throughout this journey. You're not going to always feel like it—I know. But don't let a bad moment stop you from doing the good stuff, the needed stuff, the stuff that will make you whole. Focus on the harvest that is waiting for you—one filled with wellness and wholeness. It's worth pressing on.

MY CONFESSION

I will not give up as I strive for wellness and wholeness.
A bad moment is just that—a moment.

Make a plan to do one thing today that is intentionally good for your mind.

God of the harvest: I know I will reap what I have sown. Give me the strength to keep moving even when I experience a bad moment. I want to do what is good for my mind, body, and soul. Amen.

BUCKET LIST

Ecclesiastes 9:1–7

Go, eat your food with gladness, and drink your wine with a
joyful heart, for God has already approved what you do.
ECCLESIASTES 9:7

The term *bucket list* became popular sometime after the movie by the same name. While I don't recommend doing dangerous, near-death things just to "live," I think there's some value in creating a list of things you've always wanted to do but never did—or haven't done in a long time. Creating this list can free your mind to dream and hope and think of a time you may feel better. But actually doing some of the things on your list is even better. It gives you a thrill and a sense of accomplishment while allowing you to enjoy an activity you've longed to do. It can help you look forward to an activity and give you hope for more than the clouds you currently see.

My list changes as I change, but here are a few sample items I've added to my bucket list. Feel free to borrow some, but please give yourself the joy of thinking of your own. I admit I have had trouble thinking of what I want during times of the blues. I don't know. I can't think straight. But when I'm feeling better, adding to the list comes easier. It's okay if you can't think of much when you are down; you can always edit your list later. I also try to list things that involve a luxury vacation as well as things that literally could be done tomorrow with little money.

- Go horseback riding
- Take a hot-air balloon ride

- Sew a blouse or dress for myself (well, learn to sew first)
- Skate well (as I age, this one may get deleted, but the freedom people display as they glide around a rink is attractive to me)
- Climb a mountain
- Vacation with my sister

MY CONFESSION

I will look forward to living life and doing activities on my bucket list.

You get to edit your bucket list.

PROGRESS, NOT PERFECTION

You know what this will be. Do just one thing—or take steps toward it.

Amazing God: Renew my mind and spirit so I may see the adventurous parts of life again. Give me the desire to try something new. Amen.

S⁰CIAL MEDIA DISCIPLINE
Hebrews 12:10–12

No discipline seems pleasant at the time, but painful. Later on, however, it produces a harvest of righteousness and peace for those who have been trained by it.
HEBREWS 12:11

Since my first acknowledged episode of depression, we now have the sometimes-wonderful tool called social media. I have to say, going through depression in a world void of millions of pictures at the disposal of my little handheld device (called a smartphone) was tough. But, going through any of the mental illnesses like depression, the blues, and anxiety with social media is on a whole nother level.

And before you say what many say—"Just get off of it"—dare I say some of us use social media for connection and for work and for promoting books so getting rid of it totally is unpractical. And there are some benefits to being connected if only through a virtual network.

But let me share a few words of caution if you are plagued with mental health concerns during this time of major social media use.

- It's just not what it seems. I know: she looks great in that dress; her husband looks like he adores her; the kids are perfect. I personally have never liked picture day; it's just too stressful—getting the hair, outfit, and so on together. But let me tell you, pictures are so one-dimensional. You just don't know the entire story—in this case, you only know what the person has posted. And if you're anything like me, you mentally make up the thousands of words to go with that posted picture. The person is making a lot of money (no bills to stress about like me); the husband is engaged and active (she doesn't have to ask him to do stuff like many of us do); the kids look perfect and have excelled in every subject (there's no coercing them to take an extra class or study even harder like there is in my home). Get it? So do yourself a favor and keep scrolling; if you see a great picture, like it and keep it moving. Avoid conjuring up a story in your mind; you won't get it right—trust me.

- Comparison is evil. Now, I know the Bible says the love of money is the root of all evil . . . but may I just say that comparison has to come in a close second. I once heard a wonderful sermon analogy that said you're comparing your insides (how you're feeling) to someone's outside (how they are looking to you). You're going to lose every time—especially when you feel down or blue. Everyone looks like they are having a better time than you are.

- Be careful of mindless scrolling; it's one of the pits I fall into when I don't want to do anything else. When done with the proper boundaries, I don't necessarily see anything wrong with this—there are some super funny memes and videos and some inspirational stories to be consumed. But when you find yourself just staring at the phone as you click on yet another app to see what's happening there (trust me, what's on Facebook is the same as IG and Twitter and other platforms)—consider challenging yourself to do something else. Read a book, a physical one; pick up a magazine, a physical one; call a friend, take a nap, say a prayer, or use your smart device to play a brain game (it at least engages your mind). Do something that will lead to better mental wellness.

MY CONFESSION

I will be careful of my social media usage.

Mindless scrolling can be a pit.

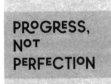

PROGRESS, NOT PERFECTION

When on social media, pay attention to the time; give yourself a set amount of time to scroll—and then do something else.

Holy God: Give me the discipline I need to utilize the tools of social media in a wise and helpful way. Help me look for inspiration and encouragement rather than compare how I'm feeling to how others are looking.
Amen.

SEMICOLON

Psalm 126

Those who sow with tears will reap with songs of joy.
PSALM 126:5

Have you ever noticed a person with a semicolon tattooed on a part of their body? It is a powerful symbol and sign. The semicolon tattoo often signifies that this person has struggled with mental health issues such as depression and perhaps even considered suicide. The person wearing the tattoo stands in solidarity with the movement to bring more awareness to mental health and overall mental well-being, as well as other diseases.

But why a semicolon? In English grammar class you probably learned that the semicolon is used when two sentences are closely related. You don't want to place a period between the sentences because you want to signal to the reader that the next sentence is very important and extremely connected to the earlier sentence.

In terms of mental health, the semicolon means the person suffering with mental illness has not put a period at the end of their story. They are not through yet. Hold on; there's more to come. Keep reading my story; it's not done.

As a grammar geek, the message of the semicolon resonates with me strongly. I've seen a few people with the statement inked on their body. I want to nod when I see it or pump my fist and say: "Right on."

Your story doesn't have a period either. If you are reading this, you are still here. You are still able to create a story that's different than what you feel right now. A period would mean

196

you're done; the semicolon means there's more—and you're here for it.

As I've mentioned earlier, if you feel like you want to place a period in your life and make this the last sentence in your story, please reach out to someone. The national suicide hotline is open all the time. The number is 1-800-273-8255. Don't be ashamed to use it. Many people are pulling for you, hoping you will add a semicolon to this sentence, not a period.

As the old church song titled "Please Be Patient with Me" reminds us—God is still working on each of us. Take a breath or rest if you need to, but please put a semicolon at the end of that sentence because there's more to write. As today's psalm says, even when you've sown in tears, joy can be reaped. Keep going; it's not over.

MY CONFESSION

My story has not ended.

Semicolons signal for the reader to keep going; there's something else in this story.

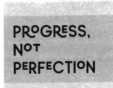

PROGRESS, NOT PERFECTION

Draw or paint a semicolon and keep it in a prominent place to remind you that your story has not ended.

Creator of my story: I vow to not place a period on my story. I want to live to see what is next. Give me all I need to keep moving and growing toward healing and wholeness. Amen.

WHEN IT'S HARD TO PRAY

Romans 8:25–27

In the same way, the Spirit helps us in our weakness. We do not know what we ought to pray for, but the Spirit himself intercedes for us through wordless groans.

ROMANS 8:26

If you haven't already realized it, I am super sensitive to the ways depression can distort our minds and our thoughts. Things we normally grasp easily and know deep down in our spirits somehow get twisted and make us feel deficient and as if we never knew some things.

One of those things for me happens to be praying. I am a person of deep faith, but when I am in the throes of a depressive episode, it seems so hard to pray. When I'm not in this state, I connect to God and treasure the moments I get to talk to Him, share my concerns, pray for others, and simply praise God. But add a depressed state and I'm silent. No words. I sometimes literally forget to pray. There are days I go through feeling awful and I have to ask myself if I've stopped to pray. You'd think feeling miserable would be a cue to pray—but that's not how things work all the time.

Today's verse gives me comfort, however, when I'm in the midst of those times when it is hard to pray or I don't naturally think to pray first. The Spirit of God, who lives in me as a believer, can turn my groans into prayers. My silent thoughts and inner grumblings are prayers. Wow! That's something to celebrate and recall—especially on those tough days when you just don't have the will, feeling, or wherewithal to pray.

Until you can pray, know God's Spirit has you and is turning your inner turmoil into a clarion call to God. Let go of your stress and shame because you can't pray. Let God's Spirit do what He does and intervene just for you. Know that your name is still called out to God and God still hears you and knows you and is working on your behalf. That can be enough to help you push to take just one more step today.

MY CONFESSION

I will rest in the assurance that God's Spirit intervenes for me when I cannot pray.

God's Spirit can interpret our groans.

PROGRESS, NOT PERFECTION

Rejoice in knowing the Holy Spirit is your intercessor.

Holy One: Thank you for the gift of a true intercessor. I know you know what's inside of me and what I need for this day. Amen.

86

SITTING WITH YOUR LAMENT

Lamentations 3:1–24

Because of the LORD's great love we are not consumed, for his compassions never fail. They are new every morning; great is your faithfulness. I say to myself, "The LORD is my portion; therefore I will wait for him."
LAMENTATIONS 3:22–24

I must admit, I rarely read Lamentations. I know it's where we find the basis for the beautiful hymn "Great Is Thy Faithfulness" (and that's one of my favorite hymns), but for some reason I'm rarely just drawn to the Old Testament books of prophecy where Lamentations is located. But every time I bring myself to read one of these books I'm always struck by God's compassion.

Understanding the setting and the scenes of these books is helpful too—especially when you're in the throes of depression. Why? Because the prophets were not preaching during great times. Many were predicting exile and punishment for the Israelites. Others were right smack-dab in the middle of the wilderness of captivity. They were taken away from their beloved land and forced to live among their enemies, or worse yet forced to serve their enemies.

Reading through Lamentations 3 reminds me again that people of faith have long endured the blues—and come through them. Reflecting on the words and emotions exuded in Lamentations gives me a certain peace. I'm not the only one who has been here—not even close. Circumstances may have been different, but others have felt afflicted and desolate—some pretty serious by-products of depression (whether their actions caused it or not!).

But in the midst of the pain and suffering, the lament and moaning, are the beautiful verses that have inspired so many of us to keep going: they're a reminder that each morning represents God's new mercies; God's great compassion pours out on us afresh each new day. I know navigating through the blues can feel so isolating and lonely, but you can use the words of the prophets to remember that God is still by your side. God is still pouring out new mercies each day. Breathe in a new one right now.

MY CONFESSION

I will use the prophecies in the Old Testament to remind me of God's compassion.

People of faith have long endured the blues—and come through it all.

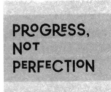

PROGRESS, NOT PERFECTION

Choose a prophecy book to read through this week.

God of all: I know you've brought my foreparents through many trials and tribulations; I also know you're right by my side. I will look for your fresh mercies each new day. Amen.

87

PROGRESS, NOT PERFECTION

Philippians 3:12–14

Not that I have already obtained all this, or have already arrived at my goal, but I press on to take hold of that for which Christ Jesus took hold of me.
PHILIPPIANS 3:12

Paul knew something about striving and I believe we can use his words to keep striving for our goals. We are not there yet—if we were, we wouldn't need a book on navigating the blues. We wouldn't need the many reminders to hold on to what we already know, to be encouraged as we take one step at a time, to do the small things that can push us toward the light.

One of my favorite quotes from another dear friend (I'm thankful for my crew of friends!) is "progress, not perfection." This friend is a lot like me. We can become paralyzed by wanting to do our very best all of the time. As recovering perfectionists, we're learning on this journey of life that we will not hit the perfect mark all of the time; we won't even have the energy nor the will to hit that mark all the time. But that doesn't mean we should stop or not even take a shot.

I believe if you see this journey toward wholeness and wellness as just that—a journey—you'll recognize that some days you will make great strides and other days you will feel like you haven't even taken a step forward. But I guarantee, if you don't quit or give up, you're still inching forward. You don't need giant steps all the time; you can't make giant steps all the time.

But what you can do is view your journey as a progression. You are moving closer to wellness each day you get up and live.

Don't let your mind play tricks on you and distort your thinking; you don't have to do everything perfectly each and every day. You don't even have to do most things perfectly. Choose one of the "Progress, Not Perfection" suggestions in this book and go with it. If you don't make it, try it again tomorrow.

In Paul's words: keep pressing. You'll get there—because it is about progress, not perfection.

MY CONFESSION

I will seek to progress, not to be perfect.

The road to wellness is a journey.

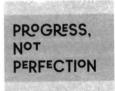

PROGRESS, NOT PERFECTION

Choose one action step from a previous devotional reflection and do it today.

Lord of all: Help me to progress. Help me to keep going despite how I feel. I know I don't need to be perfect to keep going. Amen.

Author's Note

For these final devotional reflections, I want to press in hard with more words of encouragement and inspiration, but also some challenging words. It's what I've had to say to myself in love sometimes. Fighting depression is not easy; it's downright tough. But I know it is worth the fight. Life on the other side of cloudy days is so much better. It's as if you're seeing in color rather than in gray. I know living with depression can get you down, way down, but there are also some things I believe you need to do to push through when possible.

Trust me, I know some days are not the days for these words, so please read these after you've read the other reflections that have been designed to give you suggestions and tools on coping and dealing with the blues and making it one more day. Consider these final devotions as my challenge to you; they are for those of you who have journeyed with me through this book and may feel up to doing what is absolutely best for yourself.

88

IT TAKES WORK

James 2:14–24

You foolish person, do you want evidence that
faith without deeds is useless?
JAMES 2:20

The faith and works debate is common in Christian circles. I want to apply it to your fight with depression. I hope you have faith that God can heal you; I know you've prayed about your healing and wholeness, but now is the time to ask yourself: How much work have I put in?

You know I've advocated for being gentle with yourself, listening to your body, resting, and so on. Those activities are absolutely essential to healing, in my experience. And even those things take work. If you're going to be intentional about caring for your body, mind, and soul, you're going to have to fight the desire to always work or to be worried and anxious. Even resting takes work and intentionality.

But there are other tools we've discussed throughout this book that take a different level of work. It's the evaluate-and-work-around-the-reasons-you-can't-do-something type of work. You, in partnership with God, can walk in wholeness, but it's you who will have to do that work. Good friends can bring you to Jesus and support you and be there for you, but it's you who has to step forward and exercise or be truthful with yourself and your counselor (if you chose one); it's you who will need to breathe in deeply and stop when stress wants to take you out (and it will; this is life).

Are you ready to put in the hard work? What reasons are

you still using to prevent yourself from activating your faith—knowing healing is on the other side—and actually taking steps toward your wholeness? Pray about those reasons now. When you are ready, start a "progress, not perfection" plan. Be gentle but firm with yourself. You are worth it. And only you can merge your faith with actions and do the hard work.

MY CONFESSION
I will do the work.
It's you who will have to do the work.

PROGRESS, NOT PERFECTION

Put your plan into action. List three steps you will take toward wholeness—and add a timeline.

God of all: Give me the strength, wisdom, and push I need to walk toward wholeness. Show me how to overcome any reasons I have for not moving forward. Amen.

89

DELAY DECISION-MAKING

Proverbs 3:4–6

Trust in the LORD with all your heart and lean not on your own understanding; in all your ways submit to him, and he will make your paths straight.

PROVERBS 3:5-6

Earlier in this book, I touched on the importance of not making big decisions when you are down, but I think it's worth repeating. In fact, a story of caution may be best. One particular time I can recall, I made a decision while depressed that could have negatively impacted me for the rest of my life. Without going into too much detail (to protect the not-so-innocent parties including myself), I will say that I entered and continued in a relationship that I knew from the start didn't feel right. I had red flags and warning signs galore. I actually didn't like the person and deep down I knew that. I had questioned the person's ethics earlier—before we started dating. There were some stories this person told me that made me raise an eyebrow. I think I even shared some of those thoughts with another friend.

However, when this person called me and asked me out, I just wanted to get out. I wanted something to distract me from the way I was feeling. I saw this opportunity as a way to push through my depression.

Boy, was I wrong. One decision led to another, which led to another. And before I knew it, I was in a full-blown relationship. I was still very depressed—in fact, the complexities of the relationship made me even more depressed. My "partner" acknowledged my depression and came up with some ways to cure it—and of course they benefited him more than me.

I've long since forgiven this person as well as myself for my own decisions (thank God; it wasn't easy but it was necessary). But I do wonder how differently my healing would have looked if I would have paused before making the decision to enter into a relationship. I could have said: *Girl, you know you're not in the right headspace right now. Don't do this.*

I thank God for the help I received to rectify this relationship; I still mourn some of the things I did when exiting this relationship and even some of the friends I lost (because like in a divorce, people will choose sides). But I learned a valuable lesson: not to make big decisions when I know I'm not feeling well.

Give yourself the gift of delaying big decisions during your vulnerable times.

MY CONFESSION

I will not make big decisions when I know I'm not well.

Give yourself the gift of delaying big decisions until you feel more like yourself.

Celebrate saying "not now." Remind yourself that by delaying your decision, you are making the best choice.

God: Give me the wisdom and discernment to pause. Help me to not rush to make any decisions, especially when I'm not feeling my best. With your help, I want to make good choices in all areas of my life. Amen.

YOU WILL GET THROUGH
John 16:32–33

In this world you will have trouble. But take heart!
I have overcome the world.
JOHN 16:33

One of my weight-loss or weight-management programs asks the pertinent question: Do you believe you can lose and keep off weight? I thought this was a peculiar question, but as I thought more about it, I realized it was what I needed the most.

When I believe I can do something, I'm one step closer to accomplishing it. If I don't believe it, it won't happen because I'm part of the equation in bringing it about. I will sabotage my efforts and wake up unmotivated. I will use all of my past mistakes and obstacles as reasons I can't go on instead of learning lessons on the journey. A stumble will become a motivation-ending play. Temptation will take me out—all because I don't believe that I can succeed.

Fighting through your depression can be like that too. Of course you need to apply some more tools as discussed throughout this book, as well as realize the multiple causes and circumstances that contribute to the blues—along with walking the road and acknowledging the complexities of the disease. But do you believe wellness awaits you on this journey? Do you believe you can live differently and wholly?

When you say yes, you're now ready to put into action all that we've discussed in this book and more. You're ready to do what it takes to walk toward your goal—that includes speaking the hard truths to yourself, being gentle with yourself when needed, finding the help you may need, setting boundaries that are necessary, and more. It's not an easy walk in the park. Jesus reminds us that trials and tribulations are a part of our life. But I love the second part of today's verse when He reminds us to be of good courage and hope and heart! Why? Not because we will have troubles of many kinds, not because depression and the blues may be a part of our lives; no, we can be of good cheer and take heart because we have Jesus, who has overcome the world.

Jesus's example shows us that we are overcomers. It reminds us that what we deal with today doesn't have to last always; trouble can be overcome. Jesus did it. With God's help, you can too. Do you believe?

MY CONFESSION

I believe I can be made whole.

Jesus said we would have trouble, but to be of good cheer because He has overcome.

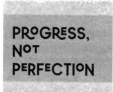

PROGRESS, NOT PERFECTION

Write a letter to yourself, encouraging yourself to keep going on your journey toward wholeness.

Almighty God: I thank you for all of the tools and resources you have created for me. Give me the discernment and strength to choose them wisely and to put them into action. I believe you will help me be whole. Amen.

ABOUT THE AUTHOR

A regular contributor to *Our Daily Bread*, Katara Washington Patton is senior editor for Our Daily Bread Publishing and the author of eight books. In addition to *Navigating the Blues*, she has authored *Successful Women of the Bible, Successful Moms of the Bible, Successful Leaders of the Bible, Inspiration for Christian Teen Girls, Joyous Advent, 5-Minute Devotional Book for Women*, and *The Parables of Jesus Coloring Book Devotional.*

She has worked in the editorial and acquisitions departments at Weekly Reader Corporation, *Jet* magazine, Urban Ministries, Inc. (UMI), McGraw Hill, *The African American Pulpit, The Chicago Defender*, Tyndale House Publishers, and *Christian Century* magazine. In 2014, she was named nonfiction editor of the year by the Advanced Writers and Speakers Association (AWSA).

Katara graduated summa cum laude from Dillard University (New Orleans, LA) with a bachelor of arts degree in mass communications and English. She then earned a master of journalism in magazine publishing from the Medill School of Journalism at Northwestern University (Evanston, IL). She also received a master of divinity from Garrett-Evangelical Theological Seminary (Evanston, IL).

Katara is a native of Thibodaux, Louisiana. She and her husband, Derrick, reside on the South Side of Chicago. They have one daughter, Kayla. Katara is a member of Trinity United Church of Christ in Chicago. As much as possible, she tries to enjoy a Zumba class and a competitive game of Scrabble to keep her life balanced.

OTHER TITLES IN THE VOICES COLLECTION

Available at

https://ourdailybreadpublishing.org/voicescollection.html,
Amazon, or your local bookstore

Help us get the word out!

Our Daily Bread Publishing exists to feed the soul with the Word of God.

If you appreciated this book, please let others know.

- Pick up another copy to give as a gift.
- Share a link to the book or mention it on social media.
- Write a review on your blog, on a bookseller's website, or at our own site (odb.org/store).
- Recommend this book for your church, book club, or small group.

Connect with us:

 @ourdailybread

 @ourdailybread

 @ourdailybread

Our Daily Bread Publishing
PO Box 3566
Grand Rapids, Michigan 49501 USA

✉ books@odb.org